PEYTON PLACE
COMES HOME to MAINE

*The Making
of the
Iconic Film*

PEYTON PLACE
COMES HOME to MAINE
The Making of the Iconic Film

MAC SMITH

Down East Books

Camden, Maine

Down East Books

Published by Down East Books
An imprint of Globe Pequot
Trade division of The Rowman & Littlefield Publishing Group, Inc.
4501 Forbes Blvd., Ste. 200
Lanham, MD 20706
www.rowman.com
www.downeastbooks.com

Distributed by NATIONAL BOOK NETWORK

Library of Congress Cataloging-in-Publication Data

Library of Congress Control Number: 2020932489

ISBN 978-1-60893-718-9 (hardcover)
ISBN 978-1-60893-719-6 (e-book)

♾™ The paper used in this publication meets the minimum requirements of American National Standard for Information Sciences—Permanence of Paper for Printed Library Materials, ANSI/NISO Z39.48-1992.

To my brother Shawn,
Tim, Kayden, and Harper,
and the Tuckers

For the film, the archway between Camden and Rockport was repainted to read "Entering Peyton Place." Here, the cast poses for a promotional shot, with Lana Turner's stand-in Loretta Thomas and director Mark Robson front and center.

Mark Robson (far right) directs a scene at Camden Harbor.

An example of one of the movie posters for the film.

One

Novel Too Hot for Vermont May Be Filmed in Maine

—Associated Press

WHEN CAMDEN was selected as the site for filming the spicy, controversial new book *Peyton Place*, the headline in the *Boston Herald* read, "*Peyton Place* Finds A Happy Home in Maine." The *Boston Herald* was half right; *Peyton Place* had found a home, and sometimes any home is happy just because it has been found. Two neighboring states had already rejected 20th Century Fox's request to serve as the location to film the movie; the towns involved in those states were split in half by heated battles over the film. Not everyone in Maine was on board with the idea of the movie being shot there either. Newspapers from some of the biggest cities in Maine went to battle over the issue. In the end, Camden was even battling with popular national magazine *Life*, which insinuated to its thirteen million readers that the people of that small town had been seduced by dollar signs.

When Hollywood did arrive in Maine in June 1957 to begin a monthlong production, the home truly did seem to become happy. There was almost a carnival-like atmosphere on the Maine coast that summer. And the state ended up with a uniquely preserved, rolling image of one of its most beautiful areas, in all its 1950s splendor, and a great story to go with it.

If Camden really had been Peyton Place, perhaps the villagers would have wondered who all those men were that their neighbor, Edith Crockett, a woman in her late thirties, was riding around with, up and down Camden's streets, in those rented cars in the April rain. In *Peyton Place*, it was not so much about what people did but about how other people interpreted what was being done.

It was just about Easter 1957, and the eyes of the state, of New England, and of the country had been riveted on the small, beautiful seaside town of Camden and its surrounding towns for the past few days.

The hot topic in the United States for the past few months had been a book called *Peyton Place*, written by a New Hampshire mother, the wife of a schoolteacher who, it was said, had just gotten fired because of his wife's book. The book was adult, it was controversial, and, due to its content, it was banned not only in many parts of the United States but by the entire country of Canada. Still, *Peyton Place* would soon become a best seller and a highly promoted movie.

Most Camdenites, in fact, did know why Edith Crockett was in that car full of men; it was now an open secret. Hamilton "Ham" Hall, editor of the *Camden Herald*, ran the headline on his front page, as did most of the newspapers in Maine, in the region, and across the country.

"Novel Too Hot for Vermont May Be Filmed in Maine." The story, originating from Waterville, had been picked up by the Associated Press and gone national.

Ham Hall and Fred Crockett, who was the managing director of the Camden-Rockport Chamber of Commerce, are generally given credit for bringing *Peyton Place* to Camden. But it can be said that Edith Crockett did a fair amount of the heavy lifting.

Edith Crockett was born Edith Anthony in Port Clyde, Maine, in 1917. She had met her husband, Vere, known as Chum, at a community dance, and the two were married at the age of eighteen. It is unknown whether Chum Crockett and Fred Crockett were related. The couple, along with their two children, moved to Camden in 1948. Edie, as she was known, took a job in the office at Camden High School and became involved in the Camden-Rockport Chamber of Commerce.

On that rainy April day, Edie Crockett, as the chamber of commerce's secretary, was in fact escorting Hollywood film studio executives as well as a Maine state official around the streets of Camden and its outlying areas. Camden was in the running, along with three other Maine towns, for the location of the shooting of what was to be one of the year's biggest movies, based on one of the year's best-selling and most scandalous books. Towns in two states, New Hampshire and Vermont, had already said no to the idea.

Crockett and her group were looking at the postcard scenery of Camden's waterfront and its picturesque village lined with cozy shops. Crockett reported that the group looked at Camden's old brick schools and even up its back alleys.

"If you are going to have a stark story, at least it might as well be in a colorful setting," said one 20th Century Fox executive.

Two

The *Lewiston Sun* says we should post "Keep Out" signs.

—*Daily Kennebec Journal*

A FEW YEARS earlier, that New Hampshire mother, the wife of a high school teaching principal, wrote the book that was banned in many parts of the United States and in entire countries because of its graphic descriptions of sex. *Peyton Place* was an instant best seller even before it hit the bookstands.

The novel was based in part on the small mill town of Gilmanton, New Hampshire, where the author, Grace Metalious, lived. The book's central plot was based on a murder that had been committed in 1947 in Gilmanton. The "sheep pen murder" involved a young woman from a middle-class family who had killed her father and buried him in the family farm's sheep pen. The man's body was discovered a year later, when the young woman confessed to a family member, who took her to local officials to tell her sordid story of the different forms of abuse committed by her father that ended in a gunshot to his back.

In writing *Peyton Place* and making the "sheep pen murder" the basis for the plot, Grace had committed the ultimate sin against the people of Gilmanton: she was an outsider who was not only airing the town's dirty laundry in public, but was doing so in a best-selling, notorious book, making money off their shame.

This feud between the author and the town in which she lived was fueling the firestorm of publicity that was already being churned by the "obscene" content of the book. All that publicity combined was sending this banned book soaring up the best-seller lists.

Jerry Wald, head of Wald Productions, was a movie producer for 20th Century Fox. Wald had bought the movie rights to *Peyton Place* almost immediately after the publisher bought the book, even before the book hit bookshelves. Wald was moving quickly on the project, most likely to capitalize on the infamy of the much-talked-about novel, which was priceless for publicity.

Wald quickly began work on finding somewhere to shoot the film. He put director Mark Robson in charge of the choice of location. Robson, accompanied by the movie's art director, Jack Smith, quickly left for New Hampshire, as that was the assumed setting of the book, to scout for locations and to visit with Metalious, who was now living in Laconia. The men looked over the area where she had written the book, including Gilmanton. But Robson and Smith received a chilly reception from the people of New Hampshire, who were in the middle of their very public fight with Metalious. The citizens of Gilmanton were not crazy about the book itself, which contained the town's dirty little secrets, being published, let alone seeing it become a movie that was sure to be a hit based on publicity alone. And Gilmanton as the location for that filming? Out of the question.

In the end, 20th Century Fox said they rejected New Hampshire as a location for shooting the movie. Robson said the town was too large for filming. Metalious said the reason the men gave was that New Hampshire was not New England enough and was ugly. Though she gave Robson and Smith the names of three other New Hampshire locations, Wald immediately turned his attention to the state of Vermont.

Anonymously, Robson and Smith soon visited Woodstock Village, looking at the white colonial houses, the quiet streets, and the elm and maple trees. The two Hollywood movie executives must have stood out in the small northern New England town. But they did not tell anyone in the village who they were or the true nature of their mission. Only after completing scouting did Robson and Smith reveal their true identities to the Woodstock Chamber of Commerce and express interest in having Woodstock, Vermont, serve as the location for the filming of *Peyton Place*.

In small, rural areas such as northern New England, fresh money coming into an area can be hard to come by. New Englanders want to welcome economic opportunities. Northern New England's stock-in-trade is nature, the scenery, the charm of the old villages. What a great opportunity to promote that resource—and in a feature film by 20th Century Fox, sure to be seen by millions of people.

But that does not mean everything is for sale.

With articles still fresh in the newspapers about Metalious's own scandalous exploits, and with a new town banning sales of the book almost every day due to what was called the book's obscene nature, Woodstock was sharply divided on the issue of whether to allow permission for the movie's filming in their town.

The story that ran in the Associated Press was more direct about the controversy over 20th Century Fox's request to film *Peyton Place* in Woodstock. "This pleasant shire town of Windsor County, outwardly as serene as the scene of a Dorothy Canfield Fisher story, is buzzing like a hornet's nest in springtime—and all over a completely different sort of story. This village is split right down the middle—between those who see it as good publicity value, and those who regard it as a blight on the town," wrote the Associated Press reporter.

"Wouldn't they like to see Gregory Peck and Susan Hayward, wouldn't they like a chance to pick up something as 'extras' in the film, wouldn't they like to see the town gain a considerable amount from the company's production crew?

"The answer of some people here is as definite as Sam Goldwyn's famous retort: 'In words of one syllable, definitely not.'"

On April 16, three weeks after Robson and Smith returned to California from Vermont, Robson received a message from Frank Teagle, executive secretary of the Woodstock Chamber of Commerce. Teagle said the town did not know what to think about Hollywood's consideration, that the village trustees, school board, chamber of commerce, and citizens were split on the idea. There had even been talk of holding a special town meeting to vote on whether to grant permission, but one never materialized.

Teagle's message read:

To Mark Robson, 20th Century Fox, West Los Angeles, Calif.

The following is the promised result of our unofficial sampling of local opinion on the subject of your proposed visit.

The five village trustees are emphatically divided in their opinion.

The Catholic church is unalterably opposed and has forbidden the children of their parish to participate in any school activities incident to the filming. The directors of the Chamber of Commerce are about evenly split, and feel that the decision is not within their providence.

We suggest you send a representative to consult further with village and school representatives.

Robson also received a letter from Woodstock's school board regarding its decision on whether school facilities could be used in the filming, the school location being a critical element to the film's plot.

The school board had taken issue with the speed with which the movie company wanted to start production, as well as the disruption that would be caused to the students. There appeared to have been discussion of filming Woodstock's actual high school graduation that year as a scene in the movie.

"After careful consideration and professional advice, we, the Woodstock School Board and administration wish to go on record as opposing the use of school property and facilities for the filming of the story 'Peyton Place' during the school year."

The letter was signed by Mrs. Beatrix Kendall, chairman of the board of directors, as well as other school officials.

"Things are so much at a fever pitch anyway, at the end of the school year, that we'd be opposed to having a film company move in—no matter what the subject matter of it might be," Kendall told a reporter.

"We just felt there was enough excitement already, and will be for a month preceding the graduation exercises. You know how it is with youngsters at graduation anyway. We were given to understand the motion picture company wanted to move right in, to take pictures of events as they actually happened.

"The board felt any filming of these commencement exercises would definitely take away from the dignity of the program," said Kendall, who had not read the book. "Also there have been any number of people who have let us know in no uncertain terms they didn't think much of the project."

Within a week of Vermont's rejection, with Robson sitting the next trip out, Peyton Place's production manager, Henry Weinberger, joined Smith on a trip to 20th Century Fox's third choice, the state of

Maine, arriving on Saturday, April 20. Instead of visiting under a cloak of secrecy, this time the Hollywood men had coordinated with the Maine Department of Economic Development as well as the chambers of commerce of the four Maine towns they were considering.

One cannot help but think that perhaps the Hollywood men operating in secrecy in Woodstock, Vermont, did not help their cause with the townspeople or local officials. To further support that notion, the Hollywood executives did change their tactics when coming to Maine. Contacting the local chambers of commerce was a logical place for the Hollywood men to start, since the businesspeople of an area best understood the good publicity that could come from having a major motion picture being filmed in a town, and the money that would follow that publicity—not to mention the estimated one hundred thousand dollars, nearly one million dollars in today's money, that the movie company was expected to spend on location.

Though the men from Hollywood had made arrangements with different officials, it is not known whether they meant for their visit to become as publicized as it did. Weinberger and Smith's first visit in Maine was to Waterville, and on Sunday, April 21, the director of the Waterville Chamber of Commerce announced to the press that 20th Century Fox was considering four Maine communities as possible sites for filming: Waterville, Skowhegan, Wiscasset, and Camden.

The Associated Press picked up the story. The next day, news of Maine being in the running for the shooting location was in most of the state's papers, large and small, as well as newspapers in other states.

"Novel Too Hot for Vermont May Be Filmed in Maine" was the headline.

The news story told of the problems the production officials had in New Hampshire and Vermont, and why.

"Attempts to film the novel of life in a small New Hampshire town met with local outrage when proposed in Vermont," reported the Associated Press.

Weinberger and Smith visited Waterville again Sunday to look at places to be used for the movie's exterior shots. They moved on to the other three towns, guided by Wayne Buxton of the Maine Department of Economic Development. Buxton was no stranger to films being shot in Maine; he had worked with Robson two summers before, when 20th Century Fox produced the hit movie *Carousel* in Boothbay Harbor.

Robson was due in Maine the following week to take a look at the four locations for himself. "Robson will have the final word as to where the filming will be done," Weinberger told the press.

Robson arrived on Tuesday, April 23, and was met at the Augusta State Airport by Weinberger and Smith. Even before checking into the Augusta House, the hotel at which the Hollywood executives stayed, Robson and the three men, including Buxton, toured the towns that Smith and Weinberger had already surveyed. That day they visited Waterville, Skowhegan, and also Farmington. "It's marvelous!" was Robson's comment about the state when he arrived at the Augusta House Tuesday night after his tour of the first three towns.

Canadian-born Mark Robson was forty-three when he directed *Peyton Place*. He had just directed *The Little Hut* for Metro-Goldwyn-Mayer the year before, and it was a big hit, earning him an Academy Award nomination in the category of directing. Among other professional accomplishments, Robson had been involved in the editing of *Citizen Kane*, and after completing production of *Peyton Place*, he would go on to direct a movie based on another sensational, best-selling book, *Valley of the Dolls*, written by Jacqueline Susann.

After spending the day riding around the three central Maine towns, the men returned to the Augusta House. They were joined by Earl Doucette, the state of Maine's director of the Public Relations Division. With the task of heading to Camden the following day in front of them, the men had dinner at the Augusta House that night: lobster, a traditional Maine meal.

Despite Robson's warm, personal welcome to Maine that day, not everyone in the state was so gracious.

The *Lewiston Sun Journal* was the newspaper of record for the Lewiston, Maine, area. In 1957 Lewiston was a conservative mill city with a heavy French Catholic influence. On the day that Robson arrived in Maine—as he toured the central part of the state and then relaxed with a lobster dinner—the *Lewiston Sun Journal* ran a strong editorial opposing Maine being involved in the movie:

> We see that Camden, Wiscasset, and at least two other Maine communities are being considered as "locations" for the filming of the best-selling book *Peyton Place*. But before residents of the town chosen clap their hands in joy over the fame they will presumably acquire, to say nothing of the income involved, we suggest they read

the book and ask themselves if they want their town or city associated with it in the minds of other readers and filmgoers.

Peyton Place is a monotonous recital of the sexual adventures of leading townspeople in a supposedly mythical New Hampshire village. It was written by the wife of a school principal in Gilmanton, N.H. and many people there, correctly or not, think they are identified in a disreputable way within the novel.

Before someone raises the accusation of prudery, one freely admits that hundreds of books are written every year dealing with the subject of sex. Some of them are trashy, and some are serious and worthwhile. A number of what we call literary classics incorporate sex as an important part of the plot. In every case, it depends on what the author is trying to say and whether he is writing honestly and objectively.

In the opinion of most critics, *Peyton Place* is no literary masterpiece. If the author claims she is merely portraying what she calls the prevailing hypocrisy of the typical small town, that in itself is not difficult to do, given a few facts, a number of rumors, and a fertile imagination. It is the lack of other redeeming motivations that makes "*Peyton Place*" just another place for clandestine amours, and we somewhat doubt if even the broad-minded people of any Maine town would want it known as the vicarious locale or such purposeless goings on.

This is not the welcome that Camden officials wanted Robson to have the day before he toured their town.

On April 24, Robson, Weinberger, and Smith, accompanied by Buxton, headed to Camden to meet with Edith Crockett, the Camden-Rockport Chamber of Commerce secretary. The group went to Lincolnville as far as the Duck Trap River, and they toured the Camden waterfront, along the Megunticook turnpike, and around Lily Pond in Rockport. The men told Crockett that the town had great charm and that the red brick and white-painted buildings were extremely photogenic.

Crockett herself said the private homes they looked at were stark or bland, with infinite variations in between. Art director Smith took countless pictures of streets and homes for Wald back in Hollywood.

While in Camden, the Hollywood officials seemed to be doing some name-dropping to help whatever locale they chose with its decision, or at least to help the medicine go down with dissenters of the area chosen. An article appeared in the newspaper concordant with movie executives' visit to Camden saying that, though the principal actors had not all been cast, there was a good chance that screen legend Lana Turner might star in the film.

Lana Turner was thirty-six when she took the part of Constance MacKenzie in the movie *Peyton Place*. She grew up poor. She had been discovered while in a soda shop in high school in San Francisco, where her family had relocated from Idaho. She was a pinup girl in WWII. She had been married a few times, most of the marriages scandalous. Many of Turner's roles were vampy, sometimes to play off her real-life dramas. The year before filming, Turner had given birth to a stillborn baby girl after seven months of pregnancy. During *Peyton Place*'s filming, Turner was filing for divorce from her current husband because her daughter, Cheryl, said the man was molesting her.

In addition, the movie studio was hyping the financial incentive. Weinberger initially stated that 90 percent of the movie would be shot on location. (It was not; the area was mainly used for exterior shots; though a few scenes were shot in Maine. The rest were shot on a movie lot in California.)

Maine's chances for being selected as the shooting location were probably helped by two newspaper editorials. One ran the day Robson was headed to Camden for his first visit, the day after the *Lewiston Sun Journal*'s discouraging editorial, and the other editorial ran the following day, on Robson's second visit to Camden. The editorials took issue with the *Lewiston Sun*'s anti-filming editorial from the day before, one paper even saying the *Sun* had practiced irresponsible journalism. They welcomed the Hollywood men.

Dated April 24, 1957, and titled "20th Century Fox Is Welcome to Film in Maine," the *Portland Press Herald* wrote,

> Maine welcomes this week's surveys by representatives of 20th Century Fox for a suitable site for the filming of *Peyton Place*. The *Press Herald* hopes they find the locale they seek, whether it be Camden, Wiscasset, Skowhegan, Waterville, or some other attractive Maine community, and are able to proceed with their work in a climate of friendship and cooperation.
>
> We are not proud of the narrow-mindedness of citizens in our sister state of Vermont, who protested filming of the book there because they consider it indecent and in poor taste. We are even more disturbed by the attitude of our journalistic neighbor, the *Lewiston Sun*, which also presented a cold shoulder to the film producers

on the grounds that *Peyton Place* is "no literary masterpiece" and "just another book about clandestine amours."

The *Sun* doesn't actually ask the 20th Century men to get out of town but the doubts it raises about the propriety of a motion picture firm's right to do business in Maine border on irresponsible journalism.

In the first place 20th Century Fox is a legitimate and responsible company. Secondly, its filmed efforts must meet the standards set by a stringent code of Hollywood regulations. Thirdly, the movie-going public is the final judge of a picture's good taste or lack thereof, and has the power to make or break an expensive production in accordance with its judgment.

As for the merits of "*Peyton Place*," we agree that it is not a great book, or even a particularly good one. But it is a sorry day when the people of a state as steeped in freedom as Vermont, or the editors of a newspaper as conscientious as the *Sun*, argue against the making of a film because the book it is based on is bad. Great films have been made from poor books and vice versa. No one has the prescience to judge in advance. As for the presence of sex in "*Peyton Place*," this was also true of the book "*From Here to Eternity*," whose movie version harvested an armful of Oscars for its artistry and praise from the public at large for its accurate, sensitive—and decent—portrayal of Army life in Hawaii.

To the people of 20th Century Fox we say, Welcome. Vermont is not typical of New England and the *Lewiston Sun* does not speak for Maine.

The following day, April 25, as officials from Fox spent their second day poking around Camden and trying to make up their mind, the *Daily Kennebec Journal* also weighed in on the controversy, also taking the *Lewiston Sun* to task. Their editorial was titled "Maine Can Stand *Peyton Place*":

The *Press Herald* welcomes filmers of *Peyton Place* to Maine with open arms. The *Lewiston Sun* says we should post "Keep Out" signs.

The *Press Herald* argues that strict Hollywood codes will clean up the filthy aspects of the novel and that a reliable film company has a right to film it in Maine if it wants to. The *Sun* holds that the novel has none of the redeeming literary excellence that has justified many a sex-laden classic and that no Maine community wants to be identified with such a trashy view of community life.

This writer's first reaction was similar to that of our colleague on the *Sun*. But something told us to think it over for a day or two.

Most editors are busy people who have to ration their reading time sparingly. If three of us found time to read or familiarize ourselves with *Peyton Place*, it must have some importance.

Actually the book does possess a few redeeming features. The principal female character is a tender, sensitive girl who leans to refinement and a high sense of values. When she goes picnicking with a lad, readers hungry for salacious scenes are disappointed.

The book's brutal aspects appear when it approaches normally forbidden portals. There are no locked doors, no privacy, no inhibitions in portraying baser actions and language. Whether this amounts to trash or literary courage is debatable to say the least. Actually the profanity, the sexual orgies and drunken squalor add up to a small proportion of the total wordage.

But they are shocking enough to leave the impression that life in *Peyton Place* is dominated by such standards.

We read frequently in the news that a person has been prosecuted for a "morals" violation of mysterious nature. Yet few writers have attempted to portray realistically, as Grace Metalious did, a drunken wood cutter turning his alcohol-crazed attentions to an adolescent step-daughter.

We speak of the extremes of wild youth in hushed generalities. This book gets down to frightful realities. Literary tradition tells us the final test is truth, and the Bible is no exception.

Many a college literature novice has been shocked to have Madame Bovary served up as one of the greatest novels of all time. Yet they went on to acquire a taste for such ribald but enduring fame as Chaucer, Boccaccio and the Arabian Nights.

Boothbay Harbor served admirably as the scene of the fantasy, *Carousel*.

Certainly Maine has character enough to be identified with movie goers across the land as the backdrop for the expurgated film version of a much more earthy, but no less important novel, one that was in fact a northern New England product.

Ham Hall reprinted both editorials, as he had done with the *Lewiston Sun*'s editorial, in the *Camden Herald*.

On their second trip to Camden, Robson, Weinberger, Smith, and Buxton met with Camden-Rockport Chamber of Commerce officials at 9:00 a.m. for another tour and inspection of the area. Camden town manager Sterling Morris, representing the Camden Board of

Selectmen, gave the men the community's official blessing for filming in the town.

After the visit, Robson gave no official approval for Camden to be the filming location but stated that he favored the selection of Camden and that the prospects of the filming being done there were "very good." Don Prince, the 20th Century Fox publicist who worked on the film project, said the Camden area was ideal because it had everything to offer by way of scenery mentioned in *Peyton Place*. After the men left, Ham Hall reported that several town officials said that night that they believed Camden had a 90 percent chance of being named as the site for the film.

And now there was nothing for the people of the state of Maine to do but wait for Hollywood's decision.

Three

The people of Camden, proud of their town, are not afraid to have it portrayed as it is.

—HAM HALL, EDITOR, THE *Camden Herald*

EVEN THOUGH what should have been a simple task of finding a location was proving to be difficult, the work was just beginning for 20th Century Fox movie producer Jerry Wald. He had to take a scandalous book and make it into a movie script that would pass the scrutiny of the censors, while retaining the elements that made the book *Peyton Place* sell.

The Legion of Decency, also known as the Catholic Legion of Decency, had been founded in 1933 to identify and combat objectionable content in motion pictures and to rate a movie based on any objectionable material contained within. Though a movie could be released without the Legion of Decency's approval, the nation's then twenty million Catholics were forbidden to watch it, sharply reducing ticket sales.

If any movie was going to get in trouble with the Legion of Decency, it would be *Peyton Place*. Besides the book's contents, another reason there was so much controversy surrounding *Peyton Place* was the author herself.

Grace Metalious was born Marie Grace de Repentigny in Manchester, New Hampshire, on September 8, 1924, daughter of Alfred and Laurette Royer de Repentigny. Grace was a somewhat socially withdrawn girl who liked to tell tall tales, a trait that continued in both her personal and professional adult life. Grace's father, who worked as a newspaper printer, deserted the family when Grace was just a little girl. Her mother was described as haughty and domineering. Laurette de Repentigny always said that she was descended from royalty and had married beneath her. After *Peyton Place* was published and was successful, Grace's mother would claim that she had written the book.

Grace was spoiled by her father until he walked out on the family. Grace had one sibling, a sister, Bunny, whom the family described as "the pretty one." Grace's mother would struggle to keep the family together, helping make ends meet by working in a yarn shop or doing clerical work. Laurette's mother had a hand in raising Grace and her sister, spending many nights baby-sitting while Laurette worked or went out. Grace herself would work as a store clerk to help her own family out in the lean years.

Grace was raised a Roman Catholic, rejecting the religion later in life. As a girl, Grace liked to write short stories and read. Grace grew up hiding the fact that the family was poor and that there were drunkenness and violent fights in her upbringing. She said she always considered herself a phony.

Grace was raised on Upper Hanover Street in Manchester. She lived near a set of railroad tracks, and her mother used those tracks as a social divider. Grace would end up marrying a man from what her mother considered the wrong side of those tracks.

After Grace married her longtime friend, George Metalious, the couple, struggling on his teacher's salary and the little money Grace brought in from menial jobs, would move to Gilmanton, where George would take a job as a teaching principal in the local school. The couple had three children: two girls and a boy.

A cold feud started between the people of Gilmanton and Grace even before the book was being written. Grace was an outsider. It was said that she kept a slovenly house and was a bit of an inattentive mother to her three children. She was known to have extramarital affairs. At one point, Grace and George abruptly packed up their children into their car and took off for the West during the middle of the school year. Not helping matters was that around this time there was an outstanding charge for a bad check Grace had allegedly written.

When the Metalious family returned to Gilmanton from the unexpected trip West—for whatever reason it had been taken—the cold feud between Grace and Gilmanton turned hot. Grace was nearing completion of a novel, and she was not being quiet about it around town. Word soon got out that the book she was working on involved the people of Gilmanton. *Peyton Place*'s plot did come from real people and real events of the small New Hampshire town.

The real-life event that Grace's book was centered on was Gilmanton's "sheep pen murder." In 1947 Gilmanton, a middle-class family surnamed Roberts lived on a farm. Mrs. Roberts had died, and Mr. Roberts and one of his sons went to work in the Merchant Marine, regularly sending money home to daughter Barbara and her little brother Billy.

Barbara, twenty years old, was described as very pretty, having "Bette Davis eyes." She and her brother tended what was left of the family farm and also kept a farm stand to make a little extra money to help make ends meet.

At one point, Barbara suddenly left town. She would eventually confess to killing her father and burying him in the sheep pen of the nearly deserted farm.

Barbara said that the murder occurred a few days before Christmas the previous year. Her father, Sylvester Roberts, having returned home on leave, had called from the bus station, about thirty miles away, for his daughter Barbara to pick him up. The family car was not running and Barbara had no way to get to the bus station.

Sylvester had been described as having a quick temper, but it was also said that he did come out of his temperamental flare-ups quickly. According to Barbara, her father had in the past threatened to kill her if he had to walk home from the bus station. Barbara stood in the kitchen of the farmhouse, not knowing what to do.

Suddenly the kitchen door opened and there stood Sylvester. Barbara said he lunged at her, but she was able to break free, and she shot him, in the back, in self-defense.

"At 6:15 p.m., I heard my father raving as he came up the walk. I remembered that he had often warned me that if I failed to meet him at the train, he would kill me. I was in the pantry just finishing some ironing when he came in. He lunged for me, put his hands on my throat. I broke away. His back was turned, I think to put on the light in the kitchen. I picked up the gun and shot him. I think he was dead right away. I had a great fear of him. I killed him to defend myself," she told the police the following year.

Barbara, who neighbors described as remarkably strong, said she dragged her father's body to a sheep pen on the property. She pried up a few loose floorboards, put her father's body in its resting place, then replaced the boards.

The following year she confessed to police what she had done, and soon law enforcement officials were tearing up the floor of the sheep pen.

Barbara was prepared to go to trial but abruptly pleaded guilty after her little brother was also arraigned in the crime. In the midst of the scandal there were accusations of sexual aggression on the part of Sylvester toward Barbara.

Grace heard this story from Laurie Wilkens, who was one of her few friends in Gilmanton and had been a reporter for the small newspaper there. The story became the core plot of Grace's book. Grace got busy on her old black typewriter, pounding out the novel that would get the attention of her neighbors in Gilmanton, not to mention the world.

"It's an odd book to come from the typewriter of a plump, thirty-two-year-old mother of three children. But Mrs. Metalious is no ordinary housewife," said Bud Brandt, publicist for the book version of *Peyton Place*.

The original name of the book was *The Tree and the Blossom*. Grace said it was not based on Gilmanton but was a composite of small-town life. The original manuscript had to have changes made to it before it was published, including changing the man who rapes young Selena from her father to her stepfather.

"Now it's trash rather than tragedy," Grace said after that change was made.

Peyton Place, population 3,675, can have a ring of truth to one who grows up in a small northern New England town.

The book reflects Metalious's love of nature and is rich in its description of scenery and how nature is part of the lives of Peyton

Place's inhabitants. The book's famous opening compares Indian summer to a woman—ripe, hotly passionate, but fickle:

> The sky was low, of a solidly unbroken blue. The maples and oaks and ashes, all dark red and brown and yellow, preened themselves in the unseasonably hot light, under the Indian summer sun. The conifers stood like disapproving old men on all the hills around Peyton Place and gave off a greenish-yellow light. On the roads and sidewalks of the town there were fallen leaves which made such a gay crackling when stepped upon and sent up such a sweet scent when crushed that it was only the very old who walked over them and thought of death and decay.

The book seems to prove the old adage that familiarity breeds contempt, as it certainly can in a small town, with families who have shared the same small area for generations. The book shows how slight remarks can blow up into a big feud. The book features a chorus of old men who make knowing comments and judgments on the towns-people who pass by them on the street.

Though at times her dialogue can be a bit stilted, Metalious seems to know the characters she writes about. She delves deeply into them, their interaction with the other characters, and their long memories and grudges. Everybody seems to know everybody else's secrets. Open secrets are aplenty.

The plot of *Peyton Place* is fast-paced with surprising twists. The main character, Allison MacKenzie, only feels sure of herself in nature. Allison questions religion. One of the greatest fears of Allison's mother, Constance, is to be talked about. In the movie, Allison is graduating from high school, but she is just entering high school in the book. She is transforming from a little girl to a young woman, with all the curiosities that go with that period in a girl's life. Through Allison, it is seen how narrow-minded, judgmental people can turn innocent love into something dirty with their gossip. Judgment is a constant companion in *Peyton Place*.

The book is reflective of the decade in which it was written—the 1950s. Everyone drank Coke. Smoking cigarettes was routine. Issues of the time were discussed: zoning, sewage, outhouses, venereal disease. Racism was only hinted at. One character confesses the secret, known to locals but not to outsiders, that Peyton Place was named after a "nigger." There were no African American characters with which to bring up race.

Peyton Place has plenty of swear words. A certain cynicism on the part of the author seems present. The only thing that happens more than the sex, or lack thereof, is gossip.

It was not just the graphic sex that made *Peyton Place* controversial. There were disturbing situations. The character of young Norman Page, the only boy who wears shorts in the summer, has an odd relationship with his mother, to put it mildly. That is just one of many examples. The book has an air of peeping into the neighbors' windows.

There is a happy ending to the book, though, in which Allison seems to say goodbye to the uneasy confusion of being a child, that feeling replaced by the enjoyment and curiosity of being a young woman.

On August 17, 1955, just eight years after the "sheep pen murder" had occurred, the book *Peyton Place* was bought by Julian Messner Inc., a New York publisher run by Messner's widow, Kitty, who had taken over the business when her husband died. Grace received a $1,500 advance.

Peyton Place was released on September 24, 1956, and was in fourth place of one fiction book list a week before it was published. A reported 104,000 copies had been sold within a week of publication. There were 300,000 hardcover editions eventually sold and 9 million paperback editions. One out of every twenty-nine Americans bought the book. *Peyton Place* would stay number one on the best-seller list for twenty-six weeks, a half year, after publication. The book remained on the best-seller list for two years.

Besides the country of Canada, the book was also banned in Boston and Rhode Island as well as many other places. Some retailers were threatened with arrest on an obscenity charge if they were to sell *Peyton Place*.

In writing and selling *Peyton Place*, Grace had made a critical mistake living in a small northern New England town—she had the audacity to talk publicly about a local scandal, a relatively fresh scandal. In Grace's case, she had written an entire book centered on the scandal, and she was going to make some good money selling it.

Returning to Gilmanton from New York after signing her book contract and receiving her advance, Grace promptly rubbed the advance check in the faces of those to whom she owed money, asking if they could cash the check for a small amount she might owe, knowing they could not.

As all of this was going on, the Gilmanton School Board chose not to renew the contract of Grace's husband, George, who was the school's teaching principal. Grace, with the help of a book publicist, added to the controversy over *Peyton Place* by stretching the truth a little; she started telling reporters her husband had been fired from his position as a Gilmanton schoolteacher, as opposed to his contract not having been renewed. On August 29 the Associated Press reported, "Gossiping Novel Gets Teacher Fired." That same day the *Boston Traveler* ran a story about the "firing" in a story with the headline "Teacher Fired for Wife's Book—Gossipy, Spicy Story Costs Him His Job." By stretching the truth over her husband's job, Grace, always comfortable with a tall tale, enhanced the book's publicity and sales.

The members of the Gilmanton School Board said that the book had nothing to do with George Metalious not having his contract renewed. Whether it had anything to do with it or not, the bad check charge and the sudden trip West in the middle of the school year could not have helped. Ironically, Bill Wilkens, the husband of Grace's friend Laurie Wilkens, who had told Grace about the "sheep pen murder," served on that school board.

Grace's comments regarding Gilmanton, and all small towns, during book publicity interviews were deepening the divide with her fellow townspeople.

"To a tourist these towns look as peaceful as a postcard picture. But if you go beneath that picture, it's like turning over a rock with your foot—all kinds of strange things crawl out. Everybody who lives in town knows what's going on—there are no secrets—but they don't want outsiders to know," Grace said in a book publicity interview.

The people of Gilmanton never forgave Grace for that remark or for airing their dirty laundry in public.

By now people were ignoring Grace on the street. There was an informal "I Hate Grace" campaign in the Gilmanton area. The police chief of Gilmanton said he would not allow the book to be sold by Gilmanton retailers due to its content. Grace's oldest daughter had to be taken out of the public school because of harassment. Grace was sued for libel by a friend whose name appeared in the book.

Soon the Metaliouses separated, and Grace began an affair with New Hampshire radio disc jockey T. J. Martin, who became her new manager, all in front of the eyes of the world and a hungry press. Though Grace was still married to George, it was T. J. who was appearing in publicity pictures and accompanying her to interviews. The public knew that this married woman was carrying on with another man and that she did not seem to care—perhaps she may have even been flaunting it.

Even before *Peyton Place* was published, the novel had caught the eye of movie producer Jerry Wald.

Wald specialized in making movies that were popular with women.

"What's wrong with having one of the characters say, 'I love you'? I'm for it—and so are feminine moviegoers," Wald once said. "If a producer makes a great woman's story, it can't miss being a hit."

Jerry Wald was forty-five when *Peyton Place* was published. He was known as one of the leading filmmakers of the time, working with such stars as Humphrey Bogart, Lauren Bacall, Joan Crawford, Danny Kaye, Gary Cooper, Milton Berle, Doris Day, Kirk Douglas, and even future president Ronald Reagan. Howard Hughes, one of the richest men in the country, and one of the most eccentric, was reported to have paid Warner Brothers $150,000 to release Wald from his contract so that he and Wald could make movies together. The Wald-Hughes partnership dissolved within a few years, reportedly due to interference in productions from Hughes. Later, Wald signed with 20th Century Fox and established Jerry Wald Productions. His first few movies with Fox were hits. *Peyton Place* was later called one of the biggest successes of his career.

Wald was described as "the fastest and smoothest talker ever born in the borough of Brooklyn." When working at a different studio, there was an executive named Harry Cohn, who often blocked Wald's movie plans. At Cohn's funeral, when Wald was asked why he had come to the funeral of a man he disliked, he replied, "I want to make sure the bastard is dead."

Wald immediately bought the movie and television rights for *Peyton Place* from Metalious, and even the name "Peyton Place," for $250,000, with $75,000 to be paid to Metalious on the spot.

Metalious considered the book to be her "baby" and said that after she sold the movie rights to the Hollywood producer, she always felt like she sold her child to Wald.

Wald said *Peyton Place* had the "hard core of moral truth" needed for a film to be successful. His critics said he couldn't make "a decent picture out of a dirty book." Wald said he enjoyed the challenge.

The process of turning the racy book into a movie script that would pass the scrutinizing eyes of the Legion of Decency and keep the interest of the public was indeed going to be a challenge. Wald brought in scriptwriter John Michael Hayes.

Hayes was thirty-eight when he was enlisted to help with the screen adaption of Metalious's book. As a boy, Hayes enjoyed reading, and by junior high school he was writing articles about the Boy Scouts for his school newspaper, and soon the town's paper, in Worcester, Massachusetts. Hayes later became a radio comedy and drama writer before going on to write for the movies. He was involved in projects with stars such as Joan Crawford, Susan Hayward, and Elizabeth Taylor. Hayes had also collaborated with Alfred Hitchcock, including on the movie *Rear Window* as well as *To Catch a Thief.* In his later years Hayes would, ironically, retire to New Hampshire.

Hayes made many changes to the book version of *Peyton Place,* taking a 372-page book and turning it into a two-and-a-half-hour movie.

If Metalious had sold her baby, she wanted to see that it was taken care of properly. She was invited to Hollywood, to serve as script consultant, she was told. She thought she would be the one transforming her baby from a book, which represented her thoughts and ideas—her original work—into a Hollywood movie. She looked forward to the experience. She packed up her boyfriend and her three children into the family car and headed west.

Metalious was in Hollywood for approximately two weeks, put up in a top-notch hotel, and treated like royalty by 20th Century Fox. Her children were taken to meet the studio's stars. The housewife from New Hampshire had arrived.

But she was bitterly disappointed with the professional side of her visit and the grinding machinery that she saw tearing her baby apart.

When Metalious arrived at Wald Productions, she expected to find an office in which to work on the script. What she found, however, was not an office but the movie set of an office, which was used to take a few publicity pictures of the author sitting at a typewriter. A curtain, not an office wall, served as the backdrop for the photographs. Metalious asked to see the script and was stalled for two days.

Metalious felt the casting was like a cattle market. At one point she sat in on a story conference.

"I thought they were kidding when they suggested casting Red Skelton in the role of Kenny Sterns and Pat Boone as the 'good boy in the book.' Then someone yelled, 'Pat's a singer.' Another said, 'We could work up a song for him.' I thought I would get into the conversation and suggested Pat could sing the '*Peyton Place* Blues.' Then I realized they really meant it. That was enough for me, and I took off for home."

Before packing up her entourage and heading back to New Hampshire, Metalious would go to dinner at a fine restaurant with Wald and Hayes. Hayes asked her if her book was autobiographical, a question that she hated. Her experience in Hollywood had been terrible, and she took it out on the man who was dissecting her baby. She threw a Bloody Mary in Hayes's face.

Metalious said that at one point before she left Hollywood, she contemplated suicide.

For the movie, Hayes cleaned up the sex scenes and the language, and the abortion became a miscarriage. Many characters and plots were completely eliminated. The characters became a little more one-dimensional without their rich descriptions from the original book.

The main character, Allison MacKenzie, is described as plump in the book, as Metalious said she herself was as a child, but that was changed in the movie.

Hayes said the major problem was taking a large number of characters and streamlining them for a two-hour movie. He wrote nine drafts of a script until one was finally decided upon.

"We've washed away the dirt, and we've kept the interlocking drama of the two girls," said 20th Century Fox publicist Don Prince. "Underneath, it's a 1957 *American Tragedy.*"

When the Hollywood officials had been in Camden to tour the city as a possible location, when they were getting the red-carpet treatment from the Camden-Rockport Chamber of Commerce and authorization from the Camden Board of Selectmen, all those officials were actually taking a big gamble on the script. At the time of the visit, the script had not been completed. The state and local Camden officials would not see the script until about a week into the filming, two months later. Perhaps those Camden officials knew that 20th Century Fox had as much to lose as they did if the script was not cleaned up enough. And there was no way 20th Century Fox was going to try to get around the strict, yet necessary, Legion of Decency.

When the script was ultimately submitted to community leaders in Camden, in June, it was well received.

"The script seemed to me to be a very good story," Rev. Roy Burchell, pastor of the Camden Congregational Church, told the *Boston Herald*.

"It is a movie version of an average small New England town with elements both good and bad," Edith Crockett said after reading the script. "How good or how bad should depend, we would think, upon your imagination."

In April, on the second day of Hollywood's visit to Camden, Mark Robson, the movie's director, said he hoped to have a decision regarding the location soon. In fact before the night was out, most likely after a call to Wald in Hollywood for final approval, Robson made his announcement—Camden would be the location of the shooting of the movie *Peyton Place*. Robson wasted no time in getting ready for filming; before the night was out, he put out a call for a steam locomotive, as the state of Maine had switched to diesel locomotives five years before, and the movie was set in the 1940s.

While the Camden officials celebrated, the decision did not sit well with everyone.

The *Lewiston Sun* had already taken a shot, just a week before, against *Peyton Place* being filmed in Maine, when another newspaper reacted to the news that Camden had been chosen by taking a shot at the small seaside community.

Metalious's feud with New Hampshire was fresh and ongoing at the time Camden was selected, and that state's emotions were raw. An editorial appeared in the *Manchester Union*, the newspaper of Metalious's birthplace in New Hampshire. A clipping of the editorial was made and passed on to Ham Hall at the *Camden Herald*, who reprinted it in his newspaper:

"This newspaper has always had a rather good opinion of the state of Maine, but it is all changed now since Camden, Me., welcomed the Hollywood filming of the movie '*Peyton Place*,'" wrote the *Manchester Union*:

> How anybody could feel anything less than horror at the idea of his home town being used as the background for a movie to be made from one of the filthiest novels of our day is a little hard to see.

Publicity and notoriety have not been the same in the past, but apparently Camden thinks so.

This newspaper has already commented on the fantastic situation of Governor Muskie acting as an extra in "*Peyton Place.*"

It is to the credit of Vermont that citizens of Woodstock would not allow "*Peyton Place*" to be filmed there, and the movie people know better than to try it in New Hampshire.

Maine's desire to get down and wallow in the pigsty of what is modern day Hollywood must seem very strange indeed to those who have labored hard in days gone by to make Maine a great and respected state. Camden apparently thinks nothing at all unusual about lending itself as a background for "*Peyton Place*," which tears at the moral and the social foundations of society in attempting to make evil and the unusual seem to be the ordinary, the common place and the accepted.

Ham Hall defended the people of his city, responding to the New Hampshire newspaper's editorial with one of his own in the *Camden Herald*:

The above article tries to shame Camden, but in doing so sheds more light on the ignorance of the critic than the shamefulness of Camden. As the article said, *Peyton Place* is one of the filthiest novels of our day, and certainly Camden realized this.

But Camden had apparently given more thought to the matter than the author, who was so quick to criticize. Camden no doubt saw the filming of the movie as a business venture. Camden knew that the movie would need extras, and many were interested in the salary.

With a little additional thought, your critic might have observed that 20th Century Fox has never yet filmed the certain scenes and details that make a book "filthy." There is enough of a plot in *Peyton Place* to make a decent movie, and 20th Century Fox, with its excellent direction and photography, would be able to produce a good show.

And it is probably to the credit of 20th Century Fox that they recognized that the size and natural beauty of Camden would be a perfect spot to produce any movie. The people of Camden, proud of their town, are not afraid to have it portrayed as it is.

If "your critic" of the above article had taken the trouble to find out these facts, I doubt that he would have been so quick to criticize.

It is easy to see how someone ignorant of the circumstances of the filming of *Peyton Place* could feel horror at Maine's desire to get down and wallow in the pigsty of what is modern day Hollywood.

The fight to find a filming location had spread across three states and several towns, and it had been messy.

This was just the beginning of the angry letters, the editorials, and Maine's fight with *Life* magazine.

In a sarcastic headline, the *Boston Herald* wrote, "*Peyton Place* Finds a Happy Home in Maine."

Four

During the next week every citizen should devote himself fully to the Clean-up program, at home, at work, in his neighborhood and wherever worthy projects need manpower.

—Sterling Morris, Camden town manager

THOUGH THE *Lewiston Sun Journal* remained silent after the selection of Camden as the site of filming, other newspapers in the state were supportive of the choice. Celebrating economic development and cultural freedom, and taking another potshot at the *Lewiston Sun Journal*, on April 28 the *Portland Press Herald*, in an editorial titled "Freedom to Film," said this:

> The people of Maine should rejoice that production manager Henry Weinberger of 20th Century Fox settled last week on the Camden-Belfast section of the coast for the filming of the controversial book *Peyton Place*.
>
> This state's government has for some time been trying to keep the economic climate warm and inviting for free enterprisers, be they proprietors of big factories, little shops, or a Hollywood motion picture firm looking for a spot to perch their cameras on for a month. We can be thankful that the movie makers stuck to New England after being booed out of Vermont by would-be censors-before-the-fact who didn't like the controversial book on which the film is to be

based, and liked the business climate in Maine despite a Vermont-like cold shoulder from the *Lewiston Sun*.

But more important than the business angle is the atmosphere of cultural freedom Maine has established and would like to maintain. We like to think of ourselves as a state where people can write, paint, think, or do business, make films without undue harassment from folks who don't even know what the final product will look like.

The silly and ridiculous aspect of Vermont's protest was that they assumed 20th Century Fox would make an objectionable film simply because the book was objectionable. To that we say that *Gone with the Wind* if literally translated from book to film would have been extremely objectionable. The same can be said of *From Here to Eternity* and any number of other superior motion pictures based on books not wholly acceptable to narrow minds.

Twentieth Century Fox can be counted on to make a decent film. Hollywood censors can be counted on to use their shears if necessary. The movie-going public can be counted on to stampede the box offices or boycott them, depending on their appetite for the filmed version of *Peyton Place*. Under these circumstances the Vermont objections look childish indeed.

We will be happy to hear "Lights, Camera," echoing along the Camden-Belfast coast.

The *Bangor Daily News* was also on board with the filming being done in Maine, as it stated in its April 30 editorial:

It is pleasing to find Maine again chosen as a site for filming moving picture scenes. We have in mind 20th Century Fox Corporation's selection of the Camden area for shooting portions of *Peyton Place*.

Some Vermont communities got up on their high horse when the film company made known it was considering their towns as film locations. Objection was raised that the movie was based on a controversial book which cast no credit on its New England characters. This is an overly-sensitive attitude. The predominantly good character of New Englanders can't be damaged by the passing popularity of a book lacking in literary merit. The story—toned down—has the making of a good movie and whether Hollywood, Camden or Vermont are sites for the scenes does not matter.

Of much more importance is the increasing interest Hollywood film makers seem to be taking in Maine. Local scenes have been included in several films in recent years and Boothbay Harbor was a major site for the filming of *Carousel* two years ago.

If Hollywood takes a liking to Maine, the beneficial possibilities are great. The state could use the added business that movie making would bring here. The incidental publicity would also help our promotion of the state as "Vacationland." We welcome 20th Century Fox to Camden and hope they will want to come to Maine again.

There were a few more letters of protest. Maine state officials were starting to take hits for their support of the project. Governor Muskie had already been publicly criticized for saying, just a few days after permission was granted for filming, that he might take up an offer to serve as an extra in the film. Some took issue with the state being involved with bringing the movie to Maine or being involved in the movie at all. One person took issue with Maine Department of Economic Development official Wayne Buxton having assisted in helping *Peyton Place* find its home.

Stella A. Spencer of Wayne, Maine, wrote a letter to the *Kennebec Journal*, printed on April 27, urging fellow Mainers to rise up in wrath against the state of Maine being involved in the filming on any level:

> Mine may be a voice crying in the wilderness but may I register a protest against allowing any consideration of having *Peyton Place* filmed in Maine. The publicity on the first page of yesterday's *KJ* was repugnant to me. There has been a slogan in this state for some time to "keep Maine green." Let's, if there are any decent people in our Maine communities, and I believe there are many, rise up in wrath at the thought or possibility of having any town in Maine picked as a location to film a story that has nothing but sex and liquor as a basis. I have lived in small New England towns as well as larger cities and I do not believe there is anything in *Peyton Place* to justify its being published. I am not at all proud of the fact that I read it.
>
> If Mr. Wayne Buxton of the Dept. of Development of Industry and Commerce considers it an economic advantage to have such a picture filmed in Maine, I would suggest that he consider well the number of parents who send their children into Maine each year to various camps believing that Maine is a clean decent place for young people. If anyone in this state wishes to give the impression that our Maine people are typical of those portrayed in *Peyton Place,* I should be ashamed of my heritage.
>
> It is not my custom to go on crusades or write letters to the editor but this is one time I couldn't keep still. By silence we condone the act. My plea is to "Keep Maine Clean."
>
> Very sincerely, Stella A. Spencer, Wayne, Maine

In a letter dated April 25, the same day that Fox officials had been touring Camden, Marc T. Greene, of neighboring Thomaston, wrote to the *Portland Press Herald* his opposition to the filming of the movie in Maine. His letter, printed on April 27, after Camden had been decided upon for filming, was printed under the caption "No Place Here for '*Peyton Place*.'"

> In your paper recently it was stated that one of the motion-picture producing concerns intends, or at least hopes, to make in Maine a picture based on the book called "*Peyton Place*," after being refused permission in Vermont.
>
> This book reaches a level of foulness, blasphemy and degradation generally below anything yet appearing, even in this era of obscenity and degeneracy in what passes for "literature." It is appalling that such a thing is permitted to be published and to be distributed everywhere, appalling and a national disgrace.
>
> But the immediate point is, does the State of Maine propose to allow something that another New England State has rejected? Do the people of Maine intend to permit it to be said that "everything goes in Maine?" Is Maine sufficiently lacking in pride, in regard for a standard of moral integrity and common decency, in concern for the protection of its youth from the foulest and most degrading influences, to submit, without a protest to such an insult as this? I cannot believe that the people of the state, through their churches, their civic organizations, and their governing bodies, will not oppose and by opposing prevent such an evil as, of its particular nature, has never menaced the state before.

Even with the public opposition that was being voiced against the filming, and the opposition against state officials being involved in the movie locating in Maine, state officials were standing strong and were still supportive of the film being filmed in the Camden area. Earl Doucette, the director of Maine's economic development, who had dined on lobster with *Peyton Place*'s director on the night of his arrival in Maine, wrote a column for *Maine Today*:

> Twentieth Century Fox's decision to film *Peyton Place* in Maine marks another milestone in our efforts to establish the state as a center of the film industry. Previously the same company made *Deep Water* and *Carousel* here. The latter, which had its premiere in New York last year, attracted more attention to Maine than anything that has happened in recent years.

To go a step further, it is hoped that the television industry can be induced to make many of its filmed stories here. Gary Merrill, prominent actor who is a Maine resident, has said many times that he believes we could interest TV producers if proper facilities were provided.

Maine has many advantages to offer to the movies and television. Certainly our scenery is as varied as anything to be found anywhere. There is plenty of room in Maine for the filming of almost any script. 20th Century Fox has been delighted with Maine weather. Geographically, we are virtually next door to New York, center of the amusement industry.

Here is an industry that would reward Maine not only with tangible benefits but with many intangible ones. Filming movie or television shows is an extremely expensive business. Before it is through with *Peyton Place*, 20th Century Fox will have spent a walloping sum in Maine and a lot of it will enrich the citizens of the communities involved. A community that could set itself up as a successful permanent center for movie and television production would have an industry that would pay big rewards. A side benefit, and certainly not one to be sneezed at, would be the presence in Maine of many of the nation's leading entertainment personalities. Furnishing food and accommodation for them, and for production workers, would in itself amount to a considerable item.

So far as intangibles it is obvious that repetitive pictorialization of Maine on movie and television screens would have a decided impact on the rest of the nation.

And it is reasonable to suppose that many nationally-known figures who would come to Maine to work on films would like our state well enough to proclaim its virtues throughout the country. Such promotion should be of benefit to all of Maine's economic phases. Despite all that has been done there are still many people who believe that here in Maine we live in log cabins with polar bears for next door neighbors.

Among Maine people who have read the book there is some trepidation over what sort of a movie *Peyton Place* will be. Even though the producers would want to portray the more lurid passages in the book, and there is nothing in their past record to indicate that they would, it must be remembered that the film must pass the scrutiny of groups which can put the kiss of death on any objectionable movie.

Deep Water has a heartwarming story of regeneration of a bewildered little boy. *Carousel* was, for the most part, a gay musical. *Peyton Place* touches on a grimmer side of life, one that is not indigenous to any one place in the world, but is common to all. In the end good prevails and evil is laid low, as things should be.

All three are vignettes of life, as we read it. If *Peyton Place* makes us uncomfortable in our vices and awakens in us a desire to seek virtue then perhaps it will achieve a higher purpose than we had anticipated.

The movie *Carousel* had been a Rodgers and Hammerstein stage musical that had been turned into a movie just two years before, having been based and shot, as mentioned previously, in Boothbay, Maine. The movie featured popular actors Gordon MacRae and Shirley Jones. The premiere, held in New York, was attended by Governor Muskie. One scene from the movie had even been filmed in Camden. Perhaps it was that experience with Hollywood that made the state of Maine more open to the idea of *Peyton Place* being filmed in the state. But *Carousel*, though it had its dark points, was no *Peyton Place*.

Marion S. Kingston wrote a review of the book for the *Camden Herald* after Camden was chosen as the filming location: "Yes, we have read *Peyton Place*, all 372 pages of it. What is it about? Is it really objectionable? What makes it a seller?

"It is about a small town in a neighboring state," wrote Kingston. "It is without plot because the author has simply woven together the lives of a cross-section of the townspeople. These people are recognizable because they are universal; the town is familiar to any New Englander because it is any New England town. The characterizations are excellent, consistent, and photographic. The writing is direct and reportorial." Kingston continued:

Why is this book controversial?

For reasons of her own the author has chosen a particularly unpleasant cross-section of the population, most of it composed of victims of parental damage who are busily engaged in transmitting more of the same to the next generation. . . .

To break the monotony of so many hapless people doing so many witless things, there is a lavish peppering of sex. The author apparently confuses sex with love, regarding which she is cynical. Thus, instead of enlivening the book, the sex episodes are joyless, meaningless, and so generously supplied that monotony continues to plague the reader.

For 32 weeks *Peyton Place* has been high on the bestseller list—that graveyard of literary excellence. The primitive curiosity in us which must know what goes on behind the green door is met more than half-way in a book of this nature. The mistakes and mishaps of others confirm our superiority and invincibility to wrongdoing. Our complacency is justified. *Peyton Place* is therefore a monument to Grace Metalious' hostility towards humanity. The book is an angry one. One suspects that it is even a spiteful one, a means of getting even with the original *Peyton Place*. It is in this area that the book falls apart. If there she found nothing of compassion, or common decency, or intellectual vitality worthy of record, it is because she herself has an intentional blind-spot. We see what we choose to see. Most of us have sense enough not to write a book as self-revealing as this one.

The scissor-men of 20th Century Fox Films have their work cut out of them. Camden wears no blinders. We have "all sorts of conditions of men" here. But let us keep the record straight. Many among us are imaginative and creative, and we watch our town building a good present and a sound future. If Grace Metalious had taken a long look, she would have found equally attractive people in her *Peyton Place*. Maybe she will learn here in Camden that she has emphasized the wrong values.

Since Robson's announcement, the focus of the country's attention on Camden, Maine, grew every day. A reporter for the *Boston Herald* visited the village and described Camden as "one of those dreamlike coast towns where geraniums bloom in boxes on every lamppost and everything looks newly scrubbed and painted." People were starting to notice the small seaside area. A *New York Times* reporter stopped by the Camden Public Library and talked to librarian Doris Pitcher. The reporter described Mrs. Pitcher as a petite lady of "traditional librarian mold, with one exception: a beautiful smile."

"We just don't have it. It's that simple. Our committee decided that way," said Mrs. Pitcher. "Yes, people still ask."

"Local reactions to the book are generally concise but unheated; the word 'script' now rolls easily off many a New England tongue," reported the *New York Times*.

The Village Shop in Camden reported that more than one hundred copies of the novel had been sold over the past few days and there was a long waiting list.

One Camden cab driver told a reporter, "What's so strange about that book anyway? Your so-called good people raise Cain same as anybody else. Hell, what's the difference?"

In one man-on-the-street interview, the *Boston Herald* reporter asked a Camden resident about the desirability of having such a scandalous novel filmed in the small town. The man replied, with some pride, that virtually everything described in the book had been done, and with more style, in Camden. Rev. Burchell, pastor of the Camden Congregational Church, with a gentle smile on his face, reminded the reporter that there is a little bit of Peyton Place in every town.

In conjunction with all the attention the area was getting because of the movie, the Camden-Rockport Chamber of Commerce ran an ad campaign in the *New York Times* each Sunday from May 12 through July 14 to promote the Camden-Rockport area. Camden resident Ann Montgomery was given the credit for the ad.

The chamber of commerce received over fifty inquiries about schooner cruises as a result of an article about Camden in the May 5 *Chicago Tribune*.

Fred Crockett, the chamber of commerce's executive secretary, said that many requests were coming into the chamber of commerce office for information about the town. He said, "This is the kind of wonderful publicity that money can't buy and we should benefit from it."

Camden had made a decision, and now it was sticking with that decision despite the public criticism. And the people of Camden decided that they were going to do it right. They wasted no time getting ready for Hollywood's arrival. On May 2, town manager Sterling Morris, a World War II Air Force veteran and native of Bangor, proclaimed May 13 to 18 to be "Clean Up, Paint Up, Fix Up" time in the town, for the purpose of beautification and betterment: "During the next week every citizen should devote himself fully to the Clean up program, at home, at work, in his neighborhood and wherever worthy projects need manpower. By concentrating on beauty and betterment exclusively during this period we can make Camden the best community in Maine. For yourself, your family, your town, I urge that you Clean-up, Paint-up, Fix-up, Light-up and then KEEP-UP."

Morris requested that any burnable rubbish, such as paper, rags, brush, and so forth be put out on the edge of the road by Thursday evening, May 16, to be taken by town trucks to the dump if citizens were unable to haul it themselves.

The Camden Public Works Department swung into action, freshening up the town, painting, scrubbing, fixing.

The local IGA also got in on the cleanup. In a newspaper ad from the *Camden Herald*, the grocery store offered: "Free to our neighbors a bouquet for you. . . . Your friendly IGA retailer is going all-out to help cleanup, fix up and beautify this community. Stop in for your packet of free Vaughan's Surprise Garden Mixture flower seed today. A regular 13 cent packet of Vaughan's Flower."

Carleton, French & Co, an AG grocery store in Camden, headlined a newspaper ad: "We Have '*Peyton Place*' Now and We Have the Best Values Always."

"Camden has often been complimented by visitors on the 'fresh-as-paint' looks of the town, and this past week we certainly live up to the bouquets," wrote Edith Crockett in her Camden-Rockport Chamber of Commerce column that appeared weekly in Ham Hall's *Camden Herald*. "The Clean-Up, Paint-Up, Fix-Up campaign announced by Town Manager Sterling Morris seems to have urged every merchant on Main Street to improve his property. I never saw such a flurry of activity as has been seen on the streets within the past two weeks! The town crew have been busy painting pedestrian cross walks on the street and painting and installing the public float on the landing, planting and more stone work is done around the Public Landing and the shrubs between the parking islands look beautiful.

"Could be we are prejudiced but we think it's the handsomest town in the State of Maine."

Despite the controversy and the opposition that had swirled throughout the state, in Camden excitement for and anticipation of the Hollywood experience had started to grow.

Camdenites stayed glued to the *Camden Herald*, knowing that Ham Hall would keep them apprised on the latest news about the upcoming filming. As the list of stars and prominent people who would be visiting and staying a while in the Camden area grew, so did the anticipation of seeing those people on local streets.

Fox publicist Don Prince announced that Lana Turner would be arriving as soon as she finished commitments to a movie she was starring in that was nearing completion. He announced that David Nelson, Terry Moore, and Mildred Dunnock would not be coming to Maine, as none of their scenes were done outdoors. There were still four parts to be cast before filming could start, said Prince.

Nathan Berliawsky, proprietor of Hotel Thorndike in Rockland, said he had been asked to reserve several rooms for the stars of *Peyton*

Place. About forty people ended up being housed in the Hotel Thorndike during filming.

The following week it was announced that *Life* magazine would be sending a reporter to do a story on the filming, along with emphasis on the effect on local citizens of the filming.

On May 23 Weinberger, who also acted as advance man for Fox, said production would probably begin the following week. He said he expected filming to take roughly twenty-eight days. Trucks with camera and sound equipment were already arriving from Hollywood and were parked on the police station lot on Washington Street until filming began.

On Wednesday, May 29, a week before the beginning of production, Mark Robson arrived in Rockland by plane, accompanied by William Mellor, who was in charge of cinematography, and the men's respective staffs. The stars of the movie were expected to start arriving by plane at the Rockland Airport four days later.

Two days before production was to begin, on Sunday, June 2, Diane Varsi, one of the movie's main actresses, arrived at two o'clock in the morning by chartered flight, accompanied by about twenty studio technicians.

Varsi did not have much time for sleep, for both she and costar Lee Philips had to be up at 8:00 a.m. to go on a tour of the H. W. Look Lobster Company plant and then for a spin across Penobscot Bay to Vinalhaven on a tour conducted by *Look*. This was the first movie role for both stars, and the studio wanted publicity. Both stars were described as looking bright and scrubbed for the tour, which was covered by local and national reporters and photographers. Later that day Varsi and Philips were paraded around Camden for more publicity.

Varsi was to play the role of Allison MacKenzie, the main character in the book. The role of Allison MacKenzie was much sought after, bringing interest from popular actresses of the time, such as Debbie Reynolds. Wald was initially thinking of someone like Natalie Wood or Susan Strasberg for the part, before choosing Varsi.

Wald called Varsi a "scared, pimply little bunny. Exactly right" for the part.

Varsi was described by the reporters following her around the Camden waterfront as being quiet, almost reticent. Varsi said she had danced all her life and had been taking acting lessons for about two years. She told reporters that this was her first trip east and that she regretted not being able to stop in New York on her trip to Maine. Though she was already married and had a son, she traveled alone.

Varsi told reporters in Camden that she prepared for her part in *Peyton Place* by reading the book six times and the screenplay thirty times. She then wrote down what she thought were her character's attitudes toward her appearance and educational status as well as her attitude toward sex. She analyzed the character's social background.

Philips said that despite his plane having been delayed over the city for thirty minutes by a heavy fog that blanketed the Rockland Airport on his arrival, he was enthusiastic about visiting Maine.

"My wife and I are looking forward to this three-week stay in Maine, and we hope to do some sailing on the weekends if we can find someone to take us out," Philips told reporters.

Philips was thirty when he appeared as Mike Rossi in *Peyton Place*. He was predominantly a Broadway actor. He would go on to star in the television version of the book.

Varsi and Philips told the reporters that they were a little undecided about the significance of their quick thrust into the movies. They said they did not fear being typecast due to *Peyton Place* or having the taint of the book put them in a negative light.

Philips rounded out his day by speaking before members of the Maine Council of Little Theaters at its annual convention in Rockland. Varsi tried lobster for the first time.

The following day, June 3, was the day before the beginning of production, and things were at a hectic and apparently chaotic pace.

The nerve center of production was in the tiny chamber of commerce office on Camden's public landing, where all attention turned. Weinberger, who was the film's production manager and worked out of a very small office, spent a very busy day before filming was to begin.

Immediately Weinberger issued a call for an authentic early 1940s atmosphere and sought 1940s or earlier automobiles in good condition. He specifically needed a 1941 Mercury convertible, any color, with a light top, in running condition.

Next, he had to check if the steam locomotive he had asked for was going to be ready in time for the filming of the scene in which it was a prop. Weinberger was told that none was available.

The next problem was from the assistant director, who asked for a plowman, two horses, and permission to plow through someone's blueberry patch the next day for a shot.

An electrician came into the office and asked Weinberger for more help getting equipment up Mount Battie, which had no road.

The sound department asked Weinberger for a truck. The art director requested a tree and permission to plant it on someone's lawn.

Twentieth Century Fox called Weinberger to give its approval to music that was to be used by the barbershop quartet, saying the song was in the public domain.

Representatives from the police department, the town, and the state all contacted Weinberger regarding how much of the town needed to be blocked off for a scene that was to start filming at noon on Friday.

The woman in charge of makeup came into the tiny office and ordered six dryers.

Weinberger received word that the man in charge of wardrobe was in tears because one of the nine cases of costumes shipped from Hollywood was missing. That case contained the wardrobe for the principals in a scene to be shot the next day.

While all of this was going on inside the cramped office, at one point outside the American Legion Band did an audition or rehearsal march outside Robson's office while playing a Sousa march. The Legion Band of Camden, having formed just a year before, had been asked to perform in the parade scene.

Weinberger had to make sure that the wording on the archway at the town's entrance was changed to "Peyton Place." This was especially important because the archway was the production company's first location for shooting in the morning, and there was going to be a ceremony there with town officials before production began.

Weinberger also had to collect signed releases from the residents of houses the movie company wanted to use. He contacted every Main Street store for permission to film their storefronts. Weinberger reported excellent cooperation from the store owners.

Also during the whirlwind of tasks to be accomplished, a press agent and four news reporters charged into the cramped office looking for Diane Varsi.

In a perhaps telling event that not everyone in Camden was on board with the movie being shot there, at one point in the day a local religious leader stopped by Weinberger's office to let him know that no

Camden churchmen or choir would be able to work in a scene portraying Easter morning services.

Members of the Camden-Rockport Chamber of Commerce assisted Weinberger by scouring the local area for props such as milk trucks, farm equipment, and miscellaneous small items.

Edith Crockett, along with her husband Vere and Mrs. Luella Hennings, had spent the last few weeks in the small office on the Public Landing, taking calls from and having interviews with potential extras. The three shared the same office with Weinberger. Led by Hennings, the trio was in charge of casting the extras and making sure they got to where they needed to be, when they needed to be there. The extras would be used in normal street scenes, parade scenes, and picnic scenes. The three in charge of casting and the production officials emphasized that no acting experience was necessary. The pay was ten dollars a day.

Weinberger told the three that a dog needed to be cast. Soon numerous dogs, "dragging their eager masters along," reported for an audition. Nine-year-old Ronald Weed of Lake City Avenue in Camden had his dog selected to be in the movie. Weed was described as being one of the happiest boys in town that day because his dog was selected.

Edith Crockett said one person from New Bedford, Massachusetts, had called about a part as an extra but disagreed with the ten dollars a day that was being offered.

"He wanted twelve fifty," she said.

Some people came out of retirement for the ten dollars; for others it was the first wage they had ever earned. There was a never-ending stream of people stopping by the small building to register as extras.

Wardrobe mistress Adean Henderson requested that women not wear full petticoats, bright flowered skirts, or shorts. She said simple clothes were preferred, especially any clothing that was period, if possible, adding, "Also bring an apron, a pretty one if you have it around."

Women who served as extras were told not to wear Bermuda shorts, knee socks, or toreador pants because they were not worn during the 1940s, the time frame of the story.

Frank Roberts, in charge of men's wardrobe, reminded the males that clothes should be lightweight. He said no Ivy League shirts or modern suits, but that seersucker suits and straw hats would be OK.

Jack Gertman, the movie's second assistant director, asked Ham Hall if he could publish an item in the *Camden Herald* advising extras to listen to local radio station WRKD in case there was a change in plans, which Hall did.

"The whole pattern of living has changed," Edith Crockett told the *Boston Herald*. "People are sitting by their telephones waiting to be called. Women don't go to the hairdresser. The teenagers? In a dither, but the girls are more thrilled than the boys. If one kid is chosen and another isn't, there's a neighborhood upset. We have about 1,050 persons so far, and we need only about 450 more."

Letters poured into the chamber of commerce office asking about working as an extra on the movie.

"Some of the letters are interesting," said Edith Crockett.

"Would like to register my 1940 Chevy for picnic scenes . . . I sure love a picnic . . . I do not care to invest any money." Roque Bluffs

"In 1935 I trained a duck, he was featured in a movie . . . also on the late Fred Allen show. . . . He has passed away but I love his famous pictures and his recordings. He was very famous and during his career he bought me a new Plymouth in 1937. I still have the car and would like to present the car to you if you want it. It is a beautiful old car and I have kept it all these years in his memory." Augusta

"Please cancel my application for background work. My fee is no less than $12.00 a shift. Couldn't work for $10.00." New Bedford (MA)

"My brother and I are from Maine, living here, and would like to know more about this movie . . . hours, pay, type of acting, and how long it will take. . . . Could our bus fare be arranged and taken from pay?" Providence (RI)

"Age 60, can pass for 40 with a little makeup. On stage at age of 7 years. First picture with R. Valentino. Have several professional songs free of plagiarism also several very good 'cold' tunes." Lewiston

About twelve hundred people, a third of the town's population, got a part as an extra. A few of the other people who served as extras included:

Erwin Sprague Jr., 13, Charlene Calderwood, 7, and Amber Mitchell, 10, all of Camden, for youthful roles.

Marjorie Anderson and Marion Eaton, in roles requiring women in their early fifties.

Phyllis Wentworth, of Hope, as a woman in her thirties.

Howard Oxton, 19, of Lincolnville, and Edward Blackington, 21, of Camden, cast in younger roles.

Jim Wentworth, of Hope, and Harry Stump, of Rockport, in roles for men in their thirties.

Alisandra Start, age 19, as a stand-in for Diane Varsi, and Roland Blaisdell, age 35, for Lee Philips.

Cary Cooper, 18, nicknamed "Gary" after famous movie star Gary Cooper, as a stand-in for Russ Tamblyn. Cooper's picture would appear in *Life* magazine with his schoolmates paying homage to the star he had become. "His back is seen often in film," said *Life*.

Ellen Cooper, of Camden, no relation to Cary, as a stand-in for Hope Lange.

Rick Ball, of Camden, as a stand-in for a child star, presumably the role of Joey Cross.

Mrs. Abbie Durham, 91 years old, the oldest extra to appear in the movie.

One could earn $12.50 a day if one had a suitable 1940s-model car for rent. Some automobiles were left on Camden's Public Landing for filming. Roughly fifty cars from the 1938–1941 time period had been recruited from a one-hundred-mile radius. The car owners selected by the impromptu casting group included Mrs. Gwendolyn Upham, of Thomaston, with a 1940 LaSalle convertible; Arthur Herrick, with his 1940 Dodge coupe; and Benjamin Starrett, of Warren, and his 1940 Buick sedan.

Ham Hall, the *Camden Herald's* editor, was called a "Louisiana Yankee" by the *Boston Herald*. The *New York Times* described Hall as having keen blue eyes. They said those eyes had been scanning Camden's Main Street since 1936, some twenty-one years. Hall's newspaper kept the people of Camden and beyond informed of the goings-on before and during production.

It was the suggestion of Mrs. Ray Goodrich and Mrs. Joe Badger of the Friends of the Camden Community Hospital, a group that hoped to build a hospital on outer Elm Street in Camden, to turn the money earned by some of the more socially prominent extras over to the hospital fund. The group had just put a fundraising sign up on their property.

Hall knew that many of the older and more social families in town wanted to work as extras but would be unlikely to volunteer. The reason for their reluctance was never expressed. Hall struck a deal in which those folks could donate their fees to the hospital building fund. Many took the offer.

"Realizing that this was an opportunity to raise money for a very popular and worthwhile cause with far less effort than other fund raising activities of the past, many friends of the Hospital have been responding with enthusiasm," said Hall. "Most feel it will be good fun to have a bit part in a movie particularly when their combined co-operative community effort will benefit our Hospital."

This was a win-win situation for the Friends of the Camden Community Hospital and the Camden-Rockport Chamber of Commerce. With some of the extras donating money, this gave a charitable element to the agreement between 20th Century Fox and the town of Camden for filming. Yes, the book was objectionable, and yes, some people opposed the idea. To donate some of the money earned in the filming to a hospital gave the chamber of commerce some coverage from those who opposed the filming being done in Camden.

As all the activity on the day before the beginning of shooting wound down, stars Diane Varsi and Lee Philips met with Robson for a few publicity photos and visited the various areas where scenes would be shot. The trio reviewed dialogue. Later that day Philips found time to himself and walked around the Camden Public Landing and admired the beautification done by the Camden Garden Club. A photographer by hobby, Philips turned his own camera on the reporters who were following him and took candid shots of them with his Japanese reflex camera. After the news photographers finished admiring Philips's camera, Philips took some pictures of his costar, Diane Varsi, with the sun, the sea, and the sky; and of Captain Frank Swift's schooners in the backdrop. Philips's wife, Bobby, stayed back at the Hotel Thorndike, five months pregnant with the couple's first child.

Varsi also looked around the landing. At one point she saw some lobster traps.

"Don't they call them pots or something?" she asked onlookers.

This being her first visit to the East Coast, Varsi said she had been excited to try her first lobster. The evening before, she had had her first lobster, the first of many, she said.

"It went down well," Varsi told a reporter.

She admired the beauty of Camden. She said she thought acting in a movie for the first time would be fun—and hard work.

The two actors did not seem nervous about the prospect of the turmoil that would happen the following day when filming began.

"They were as calm as the Camden's harbor today," said Len Harlow, a reporter from the *Bangor Daily News.*

Five

Looking at our two towns through the eyes of 20th Century Fox makes us feel like Alice in Wonderland and act like the mad queen.

—Edith Crockett, secretary,
Camden-Rockport Chamber of Commerce

THE MORNING of Tuesday, June 4, the first day of filming, was described as downright chilly, and a near frost was reported in the nearby town of Warren. An easterly sea breeze gave the air a chill that called for sweaters and jackets. The sun peeped out from the clouds at brief intervals.

Camden's anticipation from the day before seemed to have grown into an air of a carnival as the first day of filming arrived.

Filming was to begin at Camden's Archway, which now read "Peyton Place" in bold, black letters. Sterling Morris, Camden's young, firm-spoken, and enthusiastic town manager, was at the arch to officially greet the Fox motorcade. Morris announced that he, along with Rockport town manager Archie Stevens, had been authorized by their boards of selectmen to extend all facilities of both towns to the film crew.

The movie's director, Mark Robson, thanked Morris.

Robson was described by one reporter as "the kind of guy who could look the devil in the eye and say 'nice place you've got here.'"

To add to the excitement of the first day of filming, production officials announced that the Knox County Courthouse would also be used for some exterior scenes in the movie. The Lincoln County Courthouse, in Wiscassett, had been the first choice for those scenes. Weinberger said he had received written permission from Knox County sheriff Willard Pease to use the Knox County Courthouse steps for one scene. A section of downtown exteriors was also to be used. City Manager Lloyd K. Allen had approved the plan earlier in the week. He had given permission for the film company to also film some street scenes as long as the crew worked in cooperation with Police Chief Bernard C. Thompson.

After the official greeting ceremony, work started on Union Street at the Rockport line, at the "Peyton Place" arch. This would be the opening scene of the movie.

The crew had to locate a plow for one scene, and elderly local farmer Fred Merrifield donated his. Fred also got to drive the plow in a scene and deliver a line, doing it without a slip.

"It's some kind of record, since many scenes with our own crews have to be repeated because of slips or fluffs," a 20th Century Fox spokesman told a reporter.

That scene is the first of the movie.

The crew then moved to 77 Chestnut Street, to the backyard of an unoccupied home owned by Mrs. Samuel Robbins of Greenwich, Connecticut.

Later in the afternoon, the crew moved to 102 Chestnut Street, the home of Mr. and Mrs. Judson Flanagan. Their backyard was also used, but production assistants had to put up a clothesline for the scene. Mrs. Flanagan got to be in the movie, playing the lady who is hanging her laundry as the movie's main character, Allison, runs through her backyard, with Ronnie Weed's real-life dog in pursuit, headed to school. Mrs. Flanagan's two children, Sharon, age two, and David, age three, were also in the scene, playing on swings.

The wind coming off the bay was described as perfect for blowing around Varsi's hair during that day's filming. Varsi's hair was described by onlookers as a movie prop. The day would turn sunny and bright as the production crew, with more than fifty people and several heavy trucks, including generator units for floodlights necessitated by overcast skies, moved from one location to another around the town of Camden. Only a handful of people turned out to watch. Most of the observers lived in the immediate vicinity of the scenes being shot.

Whenever a scene involved dialogue, traffic tie-ups occurred as Camden police temporarily stopped all cars during the actual shooting of scenes. Observers many yards away from the cameras and actors were frequently cautioned to "be quiet, please" because of the ultra-sensitivity of the microphones. Some observers had brought their dogs with them, and more than once the barking of one of those dogs would interrupt filming.

Camden had hired two extra police officers to help during filming. The state continued to show support for the project, despite public criticism, by sending officers from the Maine State Police to Camden to help with traffic. The Camden Police Department and auxiliary officers handled traffic control. State and local police routed all the through traffic away from the business area, trying to cause the minimum amount of inconvenience to the traveling public. The highway was often blocked, and opinion was split between those who were watching the process and did not mind, and those who complained about the inconvenience.

Production staff made sure no newer model cars, "inadvertently or otherwise," got into camera range. Traffic was seen to occasionally interrupt a scene; sometimes it was a curious resident.

Inez Priest, city clerk for the town of Old Town, Maine, was almost in the movie. She was driving through Camden on her way to a meeting for the Maine Municipal Association (MMA) farther down the coast. Her car was a 1933 vintage. She was stopped by a police officer directing traffic to keep vehicles away from the filming locations. While stopped, a movie executive approached Miss Priest and asked her if she wanted to earn twelve dollars by driving her car in a street scene being filmed. The executive said the car's age was just right for the era being portrayed in the movie. Miss Priest declined the offer, preferring to reach the opening session of the MMA, where she was expected.

Amateur camera operators followed the company around all during filmmaking. People gawked at the stars.

"The Rockland and Camden youngsters are impressed that she (Diane Varsi) often walks around town with no makeup; this however, doesn't keep the young hopefuls away from the eye shadow," said the *Boston Herald*.

"To most of us unfamiliar with motion picture production the beginning looked like the utmost in efficient confusion, but the large crowd that followed the Cameras seemed to enjoy the novelty and there were few complaints heard from others whose way of life was slightly inconvenienced," wrote Ham Hall in the *Camden Herald*.

While the first day's filming was underway in Camden, Russ Tamblyn, who played Norman Page in the movie, arrived a day earlier than expected, much to the surprise of publicist Don Prince. Tamblyn arrived by Greyhound in Rockland, and no one was at the bus depot when he arrived. When Tamblyn learned that the entire unit was on location in Camden, eight miles away, he hitchhiked his way to the filming. Tamblyn made it there in about thirty minutes, where he relaxed while the others worked, since his scene would not be filmed until the next day.

Tamblyn was twenty-two years old when he took the role of Norman Page. He was a child actor working at Metro-Goldwyn-Mayer and was known for his dancing abilities. His credits included *West Side Story*. In later years he had a role on a popular television show called *Twin Peaks*. When filming *Peyton Place* he was in the midst of a divorce.

Five scenes, all concerned with the opening of the picture, were shot by the end of the first day, including the Arch, on High Street, on Chestnut Street, and on Bay Street, which included an exterior of the offices of the *Camden Herald*, now temporarily renamed *Peyton Place Times* for filming, with Ham Hall's permission.

Joyce A. Ingraham Martin, in a column for the July 11, 1991, edition of the *Camden Reporter*, talked about watching the filming:

> I remember the film crew in action downtown when they were using the whole street to film. I remember how the whistle would blow and we would race, very obligingly, inside out of sight—from the camera, that is. The camera action with its high crane-like filming equipment plus the people (unpaid extras), allowed to walk along the sidewalk made it very exciting.

It was said that on the first day filming barely caused a ripple from townspeople, and that the only impatient people were extras waiting to earn their pay, most of them in the parade and picnic scenes, to be shot later in the month.

"Fox's *Peyton Place* nestles idyllically against a shining blue bay ringed with boat sheds, dotted with small craft and tall windjammers and curving inland to a magnificent grassy amphitheater (due for a school graduation scene packed with Camdenites)," wrote a reporter from the *New York Times*:

> Water from Lake Megunticook, cupped in overshadowing mountains, flows down past the largest industry, the Knox (County) Woolen Mill (another film site), crosses under Main Street and spills into the bay behind a neat cluster of photogenic shops and offices.
>
> Homes of varying size, quaintness, and charm stud the leafy picturesqueness of the residential areas. As photographer William Mellor will mirror it in CinemaScope and color, Camden also happens to be as clean as a hound's tooth, unlike some national best-sellers. And as Mr. Robson captures some forty minutes of regional flavor on film, prior to studio interiors, the town watches.

By Wednesday, June 5, the second day of shooting, life in Camden had changed and would not be changing back for a while.

Camden's streets were washed down every day.

"Why are they washing down the street?" a bystander asked one of the production assistants.

"Looks fresher and nicer that way," the assistant replied.

Great attention was paid to detail by the production crew. Production assistants climbed to the roofs of houses before filming and removed outdoor antennas because there was no television in the 1940s. The assistants replaced the antennas after the scenes were shot.

"The amount of time and energy used by 20th Century Fox in the smallest detail that goes into the current production has been of great interest to many in this section," said one reporter covering the filming.

Jay Foster, who was born and raised in Camden, said his summer as a nine-year-old was spent looking around town for the shooting location schedule, which the production crew regularly posted. Everyone wanted to know where the cast and crew were going to be each day. At the shooting locations, groups of onlookers would arrive to watch filming. An entire street would be closed off for the day, with vehicular traffic rerouted.

"It was interesting to see how a movie was filmed," said Foster.

Emeline Paige, who had been a writer in Greenwich Village, New York, had recently purchased Camden's Broadlawn Inn. Paige told a reporter she was used to sights such as the filming of a major motion picture in New York City, New York, but not in Camden, Maine: "In New York when I was peacefully editing *The Villager* it wasn't unusual for the phone to ring and to hear a friendly neighbor suggest sending a reporter over to Perry Street or Waverly Place to catch a film sequence. In Camden, Twentieth Century-Fox wheeled in its equipment and I find myself not going to—but in the middle of—the set. Last week I walked through the stars sitting on the steps of the public library, now become *Peyton Place*'s high school. As for eating out—that's impossible; the restaurants are filled."

Stars of the movie and people of prominence, many of them reporters from popular national newspapers and other publications, were continuing to arrive by the day, and with each arrival, speculation grew about who else *might* arrive. Rumors were flying that Ed Sullivan would make an on-location segment in Camden for his popular television show.

During the first week of filming, Earl Ames, of the *Boston Herald*, and John MacDonald, picture editor for the very popular *Life* magazine, first set foot in Camden.

Life magazine had been publishing for seventy-four years when it sent MacDonald and photographer John Loengard to Camden and its surrounding areas to cover the filming of *Peyton Place*. *Life* was a weekly general-interest magazine known for its large size and emphasis on photography, and America loved it, buying approximately thirteen million copies a week.

MacDonald said he was there to interview persons who were working as extras in the local filming, for a layout in the national publication on the impact upon a small town brought by the movie group. The area was excited that he would be here—*Life* magazine was the perfect publication, with its big and plentiful photographs, to show Camden off at its best.

The people of Camden would not be happy with *Life*'s spread, though, which came out after filming was complete. But for now they were flattered that the men from *Life* were here, snapping photos, asking questions, and apparently getting an earful from people who both supported and opposed the movie being shot in their small town.

Rockland radio continuity writer and former schoolteacher Fred Perkins, of Warren, Maine, was enlisted by 20th Century Fox to help the Hollywood stars with their New England accents. Perkins, who was thirty-nine at the time of the movie's filming, had been a speech teacher and had a hobby of familiarizing himself with Maine accents. A native of Searsport, not too many miles up the road from Camden, Perkins attended both Bates College and the University of Maine. He had been principal of Warren High School for ten years, taught English and social studies at Rockland High School for two years, and at the time of the filming had been working at radio station WRKD for a year.

Julia Eaton, teacher of speech and English at Farmington State Teachers College in the central Maine town of Farmington, used the filming as a lesson on correcting the New England accent.

"If in *Peyton Place,* our nasal twangs must be heard, and our 'in's' (in place of 'ing'); and our 'idee-ers,' perhaps some of our not unmusical intonations may be heard as well, and the positive emphasis of the old-time New England Yankee," Eaton wrote to the *Portland Press Herald.*

The production crew spent the second day of shooting filming scenes around the waterfront and the town proper, including Main Street.

Meanwhile, behind the scenes, a group of prominent Camden citizens was meeting with movie officials, including publicist Don Prince, to make a request.

The group wanted *Peyton Place*, the most-talked-about motion picture of the year, to have its premiere not in New York or Hollywood but in a small theater in Camden, Maine.

The group was led by Joe Badger, a Camden resident and former newspaper and advertising executive.

Badger led a group from the Friends of the Camden Community Hospital, the organization that hoped to build a hospital on outer Elm Street, the group to which the socially prominent citizens of Camden were donating their money earned working as extras on the movie. Badger told Prince that the money raised from the premiere would also benefit the nonprofit organization.

Being a good publicist, Prince came up with a plan, to which Badger agreed. It was decided the best course of action was to circulate a petition throughout Camden requesting that the premiere be held in that town. The petition would then be submitted to Jerry Wald, the movie's producer. Badger and the hospital committee began drafting a letter to Wald, asking that the film be shown in the Camden Theater twenty-four hours before it was released anywhere else in the country. They began circulating the petition. Prince's Hollywood flare must have rubbed off on Badger. When Badger presented the letter and the petition to Robson to deliver to Wald a few weeks later, the petition, containing several hundred signatures of Camden residents, was twenty feet long.

Besides holding the premiere in Camden, the petition also asked that the movie be shown continuously for the twenty-four-hour period, as the movie theater in Camden only seated about two hundred people.

Also on June 5, there was an item in many of the state's papers that was not *Peyton Place*–related but was a sign of the changing times. A nudist camp was going to be opening in rural Gray, Maine.

By now more and more people were on the sidewalks of Camden, watching the filming. In part, this was due to the chance to see a Hollywood star in action. And the big-name stars kept arriving at the Rockland Airport. On Thursday, June 6, actor Lloyd Nolan, one of the biggest names in the film, and his wife, Mell, arrived. As soon as Nolan stepped off the plane, he was immediately asked to have a picture taken of him holding a lobster.

Nolan was fifty-four when he played the pivotal role of Dr. Matthew Swain. He was a respected actor who had starred with many of the notable leading ladies of the day, and he would eventually receive a star on the Hollywood Walk of Fame.

Excitement grew as it was announced that Lana Turner was scheduled to arrive the following week.

While Nolan was touching down in Knox County, and the area was awaiting the drawn-out arrival of Turner, production officials announced that Governor Edmund Muskie had been asked to make an appearance for a scene to be shot involving the grandstand in the parade scene. He was offered the same ten dollars that was offered to all the other extras. Muskie said he would be glad to appear.

"I'm looking forward to it and I hope that my weekend schedule allows me the time," Muskie told a reporter.

But having faced some public opposition to the state's governor appearing in *Peyton Place,* and with one eye on the White House, Governor Muskie never appeared.

On Friday, June 7, much of the day's activity was centered on Camden's Main Street. The production company deliberately chose a gloomy day for the scene they were going to shoot. A huge tank truck kept wetting down the street, for the action was supposed to be in the winter. The scene in front of the Tweed Shop was shot, in which Philips parks his car in front of the shop and then enters. The name of the Tweed Shop was not changed for the movie. The property master had dug up old license plates, including the one hanging off Philips's automobile.

When reporter Betty Potter from the *Kennebec Journal* arrived in town on Friday, she visited the Thorndike Hotel. She reported that the lobby itself resembled a movie scene. Tamblyn was playing the piano while waiting for a call to location. Makeup women as well as women from the costume department were making frantic phone calls, script directors were waiting for their pages, and technicians were hot on the phone. Stars kept wandering in and out, leaving for location or going across the street to a local beauty shop where the makeup artists were working. Varsi wandered in to see if she had any mail. Nolan came down to have his picture taken. Nolan told Potter that he was completely captivated by Maine and had only been there one day. He said that he and his wife were going to take advantage of seeing the state while there and planned to rent a car to go sightseeing. Their first sightseeing tour would take them through the Farnsworth Museum in Rockland. Both Nolans said they liked Maine lobster, and then the actor told the reporter how he had one thrust in his hands when he landed at the Rockland Airport.

One Camden citizen said, "I suppose they're staying over in Rockland so they can live it up."

A waitress at Hotel Thorndike said, "All they do is drink gallons of coffee and talk all the time about their movie."

Publicist Don Prince announced that the production company was running a week behind schedule due to weather. People did not care about that so much, though; they were still asking about Lana

Turner's arrival. The day before, Prince had said Turner was expected the following week. On this day, however, Prince said Turner was still expected, but he didn't know when. Prince did offer what he could to the Maine people, though, announcing that Hope Lange had been cast to play Selena Cross and was expected that week. Arthur Kennedy, who was cast as Selena's stepfather, Lucas Cross, was expected the following week.

Monday, June 10, would be one of the most trying days for the movie production crew and cast. The scene on Mount Battie was to be shot, but, unlike today, there was no road up the very tall hillside.

Technicians had to lug approximately five thousand pounds of equipment a mile to the top of the hill, including a delicate sound-mixing panel, as well as cameras, lights, and lumber. At some points the climbers had to go on hands and knees. A mile of power cable and an equal length of sound cable were laid by technicians along the way.

"When moviegoers see California's lovely Diane Varsi and young Russ Tamblyn acting out their roles in the film version of *Peyton Place* high in the Camden hills, little will they suspect the labor and sweat that was required of the production crew to make the scene possible," wrote one paper. "It didn't take local people long to see that the glamour of movie making can wear pretty thin," said the Associated Press.

While the climb was on, Arthur Kennedy arrived in Rockland by plane.

Kennedy was forty-three when he took the role of Lucas Cross, the drunkard who rapes his stepdaughter. Kennedy was known for his stage work, including a 1949 Tony Award for Best Featured Actor in a Play for his role in *Death of a Salesman*, in the role of Biff Loman. Kennedy was respected for his supporting roles in movies, earning a Golden Globe for Best Supporting Actor in 1955 for the movie *Trial*.

Following the day of climbing Mount Battie, the production officials had another busy day ahead of them on Tuesday, June 11, though not as physically strenuous. They shot scenes in Rockport and Camden, including one near the MacMurray nursing home for a scene between Arthur Kennedy and Hope Lange.

Hope Lange was twenty-three when she appeared in *Peyton Place*, playing the part of Selena Cross. Lange was from a theatrical family who hailed from Redding, Connecticut. She started on the Broadway stage at a young age, after her family moved to New York City. In New York Lange often walked the dog of her neighbor, former first lady Eleanor Roosevelt. Lange had appeared on television, but her first notable role was in the film *Bus Stop*, with Marilyn Monroe. It is said that Monroe got jealous of another blonde on the set and asked that Lange's hair be dyed a light brown for her role in that movie.

After shooting for the day, the production crew also had the task of reviewing the first rushes that had been returned from Hollywood. Before the day was out, the rushes were shown in the Camden Theater to the film crew. In Hollywood, producer Jerry Wald said the rushes looked "excellent." He added that Camden's scenery showed up "exquisitely."

On Wednesday, June 12, the *Peyton Place* production unit, cast, crew, all the equipment, and the associated excitement moved up the coast a few miles to the neighboring city of Belfast. There was going to be one day of filming there, but weather conditions stretched it to two.

"Hollywood came to Belfast bright and early Wednesday morning" read the headline in the *Republican Journal*, the hometown newspaper of Waldo County.

The block around the Crosby High School was roped off under the direction of Police Chief Oscar Horne for the filming.

The first scene shot Wednesday showed high school students rushing to the old brick schoolhouse as the last bell for class was rung. Robert Burns, Sandra Rankin, Sharon Winters, Burton Payson, Robert Fish, and Wilbur Ames, all members of the Crosby Footlights Club, a high school theater group, appeared in this scene with Russ Tamblyn and Diane Varsi. The teen thespians played a prominent part in the high school filming, in scenes with veteran actors.

After several shots of that action, attention was turned to the First Church, where scenes were shot showing people entering the church, the arrival of the doctor and school principal (Lloyd Nolan and Lee Philips), and the late arrival of Allison and Selena (Diane Varsi and Hope Lange).

Filming in Belfast was to continue into the afternoon, but the clear, blue sky became overcast and shooting was held up. The production crew tried to outlast the gloomy sky, but unfortunately the sun did not shine again in the morning and rains eventually forced cancellation of the day's activities in Belfast.

Arrangements were made for the film company to return to Belfast the following morning to complete shooting. The first scene shot Thursday was the continuation of the church arrival scene of the previous day.

Twenty or more Belfast residents were extras in a scene showing the people of Peyton Place going to church.

Cameras were next moved to the area of the high school, where several shots were taken, once again utilizing the Crosby Footlights Club members and other students.

The second major high school scene utilized all the Footlights members who had been signed for the filming. It was a scene showing students leaving school and the arrival of the new principal. The students had to show curiosity and interest as they saw the new principal for the first time. Most of the movie actors were used in this scene also.

Still another scene filmed Thursday in Belfast was the entrance of the local telephone company office, which had assumed the appearance of the entrance to the Peyton Place Hospital. Two Belfast women, Betty Caswell and June Roberts, were used as extras in a scene with Lloyd Nolan that showed a nurse going off duty. A final scene using Belfast residents was taken along Church Street; it was a street scene in front of the high school, with the Belfast extras walking along the sidewalk.

Among the several Belfast residents who were used as extras were several youngsters. Playing important roles behind the scenes in connection with the filming in Belfast were Mary Faulkingham, who was in charge of casting extras for the adults used in the movie, and Albert Weymouth Jr., Crosby High's drama director, who lined up the students to be used in the high school scenes.

Russ Tamblyn, popular with the teenage group, spent much of the lunch hour Thursday entertaining the students in the high school auditorium by playing the piano.

Hundreds of local residents took a few moments of time from their regular duties to witness the movie company at work. Autograph seekers found a welcome reception from all the actors connected with the movie, and many autographs were collected. Teachers, who were involved in averaging grades for the year, found the event was very distracting, and more than one teacher took time out to view the scene in front of the school.

At one time four or five teachers were looking out an open window of Crosby High School when an assistant director shouted to them to smile pretty. Teachers disappeared from the window only to appear a few moments later in greater numbers.

"All in all, it was an event that Belfast residents will long remember. Some people found that Hollywood glamour was not all they had thought it to be, while others gained a tremendous respect for the patience involved by the directors working with so many different people in bringing to the public an hour or so of screen entertainment," wrote the reporter for the *Republican Journal*.

Among the Belfast high school students who acted as extras were Frank Baker, Nelson Marshall, Burton Payson, Nancy Grady, Robert Burns, Keith Patten, Jane Kapiloff, Sue Clark, Sharon Winters, Wilbur Ames, Marjorie Roberts, James Halwey, Linda McCarthy, Judy Randall, Robert Fish, Sandra Dorsky, Emily Orchard, Herman Barr, Arthur Downing, Louise Higgins, Sandra Rankin, Leah Sterns, Connie Ebert, Betty Buzzell, Barbara Sinclair, Lucille Parker, and Carolyn Vickery.

Among the buildings filmed were Crosby High School, "Peyton Place High" in the movie; the First Church, the "Peyton Place Congregational Church"; and the local office of the New England Telephone and Telegraph Company, "Peyton Place Hospital."

The *Republican Journal* made note that the reporter from *Life* magazine, John MacDonald, had also come to Belfast, to do a story on the effect of the movie on the surrounding communities. The *Life* photographer took pictures of members of the Footlight Club, and several members were interviewed by MacDonald.

Following the filming in Belfast, the traveling carnival left for Lincolnville, in between Belfast and Camden, where they were to complete their day's work shooting scenes in a wooded area.

With production taking place in Belfast for two days, there was a temporary lull in Camden.

Fred Crockett reminded folks of getting things back to normal after the movie company left.

"With all the glamor and glitter of a Hollywood setting for *Peyton Place*, let's not forget our Donut Festival to be held this summer on

Saturday, August 17th," wrote Crockett in the chamber's weekly column that ran in the *Camden Herald*.

Fred Crockett was the managing director of the Camden-Rockport Chamber of Commerce and would be in charge of the Donut Festival. Fred E. Crockett was born July 13, 1911, in Rockland, the son of David E. and Mary Gregory Crockett. His family moved to Camden in 1916, where his father was manager of Crockett's 5 & 10 Cent Store. Fred graduated from Camden High School in 1929.

He attended Bentley College in Boston as well as Boston University, where he was active in theatricals and was a drum major. Perhaps it was his time in theater productions that would make him open to the possibility of *Peyton Place* being filmed in Camden.

He returned to Camden, married his wife, Beulah, and became active in the family store. He devoted much time to the Boy Scouts and served in many civic organizations, including the chamber of commerce. He was a member of the Gala Days, a finance campaign to raise funds for the Camden Hospital.

It was during *Peyton Place*'s filming that Fred was named as the executive secretary for the Camden-Rockport Chamber of Commerce.

"A chamber of commerce has only one reason for existence, and that is to make the community a better place to work, play, or live in," said Crockett in his column.

On Sunday, June 16, *Peyton Place*'s cast and crew went on a cruise aboard a sardine carrier out of Port Clyde. Samuel Zwecker, owner of the Port Clyde Packing Company, took them out on one of his carriers to Monhegan Island and then to Boothbay. Maine was in the middle of a three-day heat wave that had sent temperatures into the nineties, and being on water must have felt refreshing to the tired cast and crew.

The following day, Monday, June 17, a cool air mass from Canada moved into Maine in the evening, breaking the three-day heat wave. The change in weather must have been a welcome relief to the local and national reporters who were going to spend this day being filmed for a scene in the movie.

Filming of the scene was going to take place at the Whitehall Inn, in Camden. The scene was to be shot on the porch outside the Edna

St. Vincent Millay music room, where the famous poet once recited her verses. The reporters played reporters covering the trial of Selena Cross, accused of murdering her stepfather. Included was Ham Hall, of the *Camden Herald*; Ed McKeon, of the Rockland *Courier-Gazette*; John Montgomery, of Camden, a former White House correspondent; and Joseph Badger, of Camden, the former newspaper and advertising executive who had been negotiating with Don Prince to have *Peyton Place* hold its premiere in Camden. Other Maine reporters included Len Harlow, of the *Bangor Daily News*, and Jim Moore, of the *Portland Press Herald and Sunday Telegram*. John MacDonald of *Life* magazine, also appeared in the scene. After the blow-up between Camden and *Life* magazine a few months after this scene was shot, it would seem ironic that MacDonald appeared in the movie at all.

Robson gave three of the reporters—Moore, Harlow, and McKeon—brief lines. Robson told them what he wanted them to convey and let them put it in their own words, which Robson would either approve of or disapprove of. A stenographer recorded the new dialogue.

The scene was rehearsed three times and there were five takes.

"Robson led them through their scene waving his arms with the enthusiasm of an orchestra leader," wrote the Associated Press.

Robson complimented the reporters on looking and sounding like newsmen.

As the reporters were shooting their scene, a news story ran in Maine and across the country that Terry Moore, who was in the film *Peyton Place* but not expected to appear in Maine, had filed for divorce because of her husband's gambling and "notorious association with other women."

Tuesday and Wednesday, June 18 and 19, were exciting days in Camden: one of the movie's biggest scenes—the Labor Day parade and picnic—would now be filmed. These were the scenes in which most of the extras would get their chance at fame, and their ten dollars.

The weather was hot and sunny. One reporter noted that the children and adults had a triple field day that day: they heard a band concert, watched a parade, mingled with the stars at a picnic lunch—and got paid for all of it.

Camden was decorated in red, white, and blue. Huge gold leaf signs that converted the Knox Woolen Company to the "Harrington

Mills" were unveiled, and a bunting-draped reviewing stand was set up near the Megunticook River Dam that supplied power for the mill.

Main Street traffic was rerouted by police officers. Filming was undertaken on Main Street by the Megunticook River, behind the Knox Woolen Mill buildings and at the Camden Public Landing. More than fifteen hundred residents were there for the crowd shots of the holiday parade and picnic scenes, with only 574 being paid extras; the rest just came to watch. The cost to the studio for that day's filming was over $7,000. Some scenes shot during the day would be used as night scenes through special effects.

Playing for numerous takes was the Camden American Legion Band, all decked out in caps bearing the words "Peyton Place American Legion Band." Even the band's bass drum bore the same legend.

"Well, it seems Camden's Legion Band has gone 'Hollywood' on us, least wise as long as Hollywood has come to Camden," wrote Ham Hall. "Oh well, variety is the spice of life and the boys will take it all in step—stride that is."

Even though Lewiston and Camden had quarreled over the film being shot in Camden, Lewiston's twenty-five-piece Le Montagnard marching band also appeared in the parade scenes.

The female sextet that appeared in the picnic scenes had a trick played on them by Robson during filming. The sextet had spent weeks rehearsing the song they were going to sing for the movie, only to have filmmakers change the agreed-upon song to a different one at the last minute. Robson said he wanted the singers to sound unrehearsed.

Nine-year-old Jay Foster was one of the extras who marched in the parade scene along with the rest of his Cub Scout troop. He and the rest of the boys, along with other extras in the parade scene, marshaled up behind the war monument at the top of Main Street. Foster said he had no contact with movie officials directly but instead took instruction from his Cub Scout leaders, including Gil Jaeger, troop leader, and Barbara Ball, den mother.

"It was a very, very, very hot day," said Foster.

In the heat, they marched four times for four different takes. At the end of the last take, the extras were treated to ice cream cones. Foster chose maple walnut.

One of Foster's most prominent memories of that day was of Yorkie the Clown.

Yorkie the Clown was a fixture in Camden. Erskine "Yorkie" York was born in Rockland in 1892. He had a hot dog stand on Elm Street, which he later expanded to Yorkie's Diner on Chestnut Street. In his younger years Yorkie had been a circus clown. Foster remembers Yorkie having been with the Barnum & Bailey Circus. For years Yorkie had marched in various civic Camden parades. The filming of the parade scene in *Peyton Place* seemed tailor-made for Yorkie.

"I don't remember a holiday or special parade that Yorkie wasn't in," said Foster.

A heavy fog rolled in that evening, but production officials said the filming of the scenes of games and other activities would continue the next day if the fog lifted.

The fog did lift, and on Wednesday the picnic scenes continued to be filmed at the Public Landing while crewmen dished out refreshments to the crowds, about five hundred and fifty paid extras included. Popcorn and lollipops were given to the children.

On Wednesday it was evident that the heat and sun of the previous day had left their mark.

"There were a great number of red faces about town Wednesday, but most people seemed to have fun and many discovered that it is exhausting doing what at the time seems to be comparatively nothing," reported Ham Hall.

"The patience of the crowds of extras, the good nature of the director, his assistants and other technical crew were interesting to watch," said the *Camden Herald*.

On Thursday, June 20, the high school graduation scene and the Easter morning service scene were filmed. A call went out for three hundred extras to report to the Camden Amphitheater for shooting. Past and present students of the high schools in Camden and Rockport were used in the graduation scene.

With the big scenes finished and production starting to wind down, David Montgomery, on behalf of the Camden-Rockport Chamber of Commerce, invited the movie company's actors and crew to a fish chowder dinner at the Camden Outing Club that evening.

David, along with his wife, Ann Stuart Montgomery, who had a month before designed the campaign ad promoting the town of

Camden for the *New York Times*, had appeared in the mob scene at the Public Landing.

The location of the dinner was somewhat legendary. The Camden Outing Club was known as the place where Maine governor Sumner Sewall, of Bath, showed a group of inland newspaper editors just how to eat a Maine lobster. The governor picked up his lobster from the table, walked outside to a rock on the beach, and proceeded to crack the lobster open and eat it. Soon the inland reporters were doing the same.

Everett Grieve and his Old New Englanders provided the music for the stars and crew of *Peyton Place* and invited guests. Marion Hopkins prepared the chowder, and one of the movie's actresses came to the kitchen and asked Hopkins for the recipe. She wrote it down and told the actress that her family back in Hollywood had a treat in store.

The master of ceremonies that evening was Alex Gillmor, whose wife, Hope, was the secretary of the Camden Public Library. Realizing that everyone had already put in a hard day of filming at the Camden Amphitheater, Gillmor made sure all speeches were short and sweet.

Charlie Merritt, of the Knox Woolen Company, presented Robson with a Knox Woolen blanket. Joe Badger read the letter from the Friends of the Camden Community Hospital addressed to movie producer Jerry Wald requesting Camden be chosen as the location for the movie's premiere. The letter included the twenty-foot-long petition that had been signed by more than five hundred citizens representing a cross section of the area. The letter and petition were turned over to Robson, who said he would deliver it personally to Wald and that he, Robson, hoped to be coming to Camden for the premiere.

There was some disappointment in the area that day when it was announced that Lana Turner would not be coming to Maine for filming after all. All scenes involving Turner in Camden, the studio said, were done by her stand-in, Loretta Thomas. All other filming involving Turner would be done in Hollywood. Turner was in Palm Springs when the announcement was made. No reason was given, though it was not known at the time that Turner was involved in a messy divorce with her then-current husband, with accusations of molestation made against the husband by Turner's daughter.

It was also announced that the location crew was due to finish shooting in two days.

Still full from the fish chowder dinner the night before, the movie company's actors and crew attended a lobster bake at the Crescent Beach Inn, in Owls Head, on Friday, June 21. It was hosted by members of the Rockland Chamber of Commerce.

By June 27 the entire cast had left the Camden area, leaving just some of the production crew to shoot a few more exterior shots. It was believed that several hundred thousand dollars was spent in the area by the film company during its stay.

Robson was said to be impressed at the easygoing manner of the Camden-area people. Through Ham Hall at the *Camden Herald*, Robson extended his thanks to the Camden community for their efforts and patience.

"The enthusiasm and cooperation of everyone was marvelous," said Robson. "All of us from Hollywood are delighted with the great help and wonderful Maine hospitality we have experienced during our stay in Camden."

The *Camden Herald* thanked the people of Camden for their participation and patience during production. Hall called the cast and crew from 20th Century Fox friendly and courteous. He said the crew seemed to go out of its way to cause as little inconvenience as possible. He praised the cast for signing thousands of autographs between scenes. He praised the working crew's patience when great numbers of people asked questions, or some accidentally got in the way. Hall reflected the temporary void left by the exit of the movie company:

> After the past two and one-half weeks of excitement and congestion which accompanied the taking of many scenes for the first major moving picture ever located in this town, Camden seems unusually quiet. Like a family that has just staged a large wedding, a great many Townspeople are quite exhausted.
>
> To many of us who have lived in these parts for quite a few years the making of a moving picture film has been something that has not concerned us very much. Until recently we have taken it for granted, but those of us now have taken a few minutes to stand on

the side lines during the last weeks watching the development of *Peyton Place*—like the solving of a jig saw puzzle—the action has been interesting, amusing, confusing and fun.

Just about everyone we have talked with the past two weeks about the filming of *Peyton Place* in our community, those who worked with 20th Century Fox in various capacities and those who only watched the excitement from the side lines seemed to be in complete agreement on one thing.

Never has a more courteous or a more friendly group descended on this community.

The directors and technical crew seemed to go out of their way to see to it that as little inconvenience as possible was caused during the two weeks they were with us.

Members of the cast at lulls between rehearsals showed rare patience when asked to sign thousands of autographs by a swarming number of young and not so young.

The attitude of the working crew was obvious to all of us on the side lines. Their friendliness to the great numbers who asked questions or unintentionally got in the way was noticeable.

During this past week we have met quite a few people both in and out of the motion picture industry who we would never had known . . . [so] we feel that our horizon has been somewhat extended as a result of those contributes and we feel theirs has also as the result of the friendliness shown by those they have met in Camden.

We feel that our community has benefitted from this experience in more ways than the publicity we have received and the money that has been left with us. It is a healthy thing to have misconceptions corrected and we believe that there are a great many who have welcomed this opportunity, through such excellent public relations, to do so.

The Rockland *Courier-Gazette* shared its impression of the movie's filming: "Like Alice in Wonderland who stumbled through a looking glass into a fairyland, Camden citizens were awed these past three weeks by this new community, born out of a much talked of novel by Grace Metalious and brought to life by the filmland magic of Hollywood's 20th Century Fox camera crews, technicians and staff of directors."

In her column for the chamber of commerce, Edith Crockett continued the Alice in Wonderland comparison: "Looking at our two towns through the eyes of 20th Century Fox makes us feel like Alice in Wonderland and act like the mad queen."

"This place takes things in stride," Hall told a *New York Times* reporter during filming. "A lot of us have lived here long enough to know the same things go on in Camden as in the rest of the world. Most folks seemed to agree on one thing, whatever they thought of the book; when they started shooting our town in color, they couldn't resist the scenery."

Six

There were cries of indignation and letters of protest to the town manager. But most Camdenites were having too much fun playing movie actor to pay much mind.

—*Life* MAGAZINE

ON MONDAY, July 8, the last of the movie production crew left Camden, having completed the shooting of final exterior scenes for the film the previous day. When the cast had left on June 23, there were only about four days of filming left for the crew, but foggy mornings and rain kept the cameramen idle most of the time.

After filming was completed, John Montgomery, one of the most active extras in *Peyton Place*, and Rudolf Kudlich, another extra, turned over a money bag containing $568.25 of extras' pay to Mrs. Earle Pitman, president of the Friends of the Camden Community Hospital. This amount represented one or more days' pay given to forty-three men, women, and children, who then voluntarily contributed the money to benefit the planned Camden Hospital.

On July 28, a month after filming had wrapped up and the stars had left, while the town was waiting for Jerry Wald in Hollywood to decide whether to have the actual premiere in Camden, the town decided to have its own premiere.

A committee consisting of Mr. and Mrs. Langdon Haltermann, Mr. and Mrs. Raymond Goodrich, Mr. and Mrs. John Montgomery, and Mr. and Mrs. Hamilton Hall went through all the reels of motion pictures and hundreds of color slides made by amateur photographers and newspapermen in the area during filming to make their own production. The committee's final product for the premiere was called "Amateur *Peyton Place*."

The event was an invitation benefit for the Camden Community Hospital Fund. It was held in conjunction with a social evening at the Camden Outing Club's Snow Bowl Lodge.

On August 22 Don Prince sent a thank-you letter to the Camden-Rockport Chamber of Commerce, thanking them from the cast and crew for the fish chowder dinner at the Outing Club.

On the same day that Prince sent the chamber of commerce the thank-you letter, Ham Hall wrote a small news item in his paper. The piece had to do with the much-anticipated *Life* magazine story. The people of Camden knew that there would be a big story and pictures in *Life* about the filming of their town and had looked forward to the publication of that story since they heard *Life* was sending a reporter and photographer. The reporter and photographer, John MacDonald and John Loengard, had been everywhere, talking to everyone. Fred Crockett had even publicly thanked MacDonald for his "excellent cooperation." The people of Camden waited eagerly to see if their faces had been captured, the same reason they were excited to see the finished movie in a few months.

Hall gave the people of Camden a warning that they might be, at the least, disappointed in *Life*'s story.

Hall said he had seen the proof sheets of the upcoming August 26 edition of *Life* magazine's long-awaited issue. Hall said those who had looked forward to that story would be most disappointed in the picture editor's selection. Hall also took issue with the written portion of the story. "Editorially the implication of the article seems to be that the only reason the filming of this controversial picture was tolerated in this Town was solely because of the money left as extra fees," said Hall, breaking the news to the people of Camden.

Hall criticized *Life* for not showing a crowd scene in front of the Knox Woolen Mill, the parade on Main Street, the Labor Day celebration on the waterfront, or the graduation filmed at the Amphitheater:

"A more truthful impression that the co-operation and interest in Camden as general would have been provided. Instead a full page was devoted to a picture of an alumni banquet in Rockport which to us seemed to have little connection with the actual account of Camden's reaction to the undertaking."

The *Life* magazine story regarding the filming of *Peyton Place*, and the reaction of the people of the area, hit newsstands and mailboxes a few days later. The story contained many large, captioned pictures in the article spread across several pages. The story, at the beginning of the spread, was brief:

Amidst Adulation, A Note of Protestation.

The movie company came cautiously to Camden, Maine this summer. All 20th Century Fox wanted to do was spread $100,000 or so around among the townspeople and in return use a little local scenery and about a third of the town's 3,700 people to make a movie of *Peyton Place,* a novel that hit No. 1 on U.S. best-selling lists for most of the past year. *Peyton Place* tells scandalous things about a little New England town a lot like Camden and there was worry about what Camden folk would think of it.

The movie people need not have worried. On demand for $10 a day per man—mobs turned out for movie parades and picnics. For $2.50 extra to the owners the streets were filled with twenty-year-old automobiles. Camden produced boys, old men, women with children, dogs, a male quartet, a female sextet and a retired sea captain who puts ships in bottles.

Then more people began to read this novel of rape, murder and suicide and their hair stood on end at the role Camden was playing. There were cries of indignation and letters of protest to the town manager. But most Camdenites were having too much fun playing movie actor to pay much mind.

The implication of the story was that the people of Camden had gotten so wrapped in the glitz of the stars, the moviemaking, and the money that they had not realized until too late what the book that the movie was based on was all about.

This was simply untrue. Though he had been in favor of the movie being filmed in Camden, Hall himself had published in his newspaper the good, the bad, and the ugly about the book; the difficulty finding a location for shooting the movie; and why there had been that difficulty. For a book that had received so much publicity, it is hard to say the people in Camden, or anywhere in the United States, did not know what *Peyton Place* was about.

Hall said that the town was "stirred to wrath" over the *Life* magazine article.

Town Manager Sterling Morris wrote a letter of protestation to *Life*, which the magazine ran:

Town Playing a Part

Sirs:

Needless to say, "A Town Playing A Part" (*Life*, Aug. 26) reacted on the good people of Camden, Maine like gunpowder. Either the photographer or the editors of LIFE failed miserably to convey the atmosphere of congeniality that prevails here.

The so-called "mobs" that you mentioned who volunteered as "extras" did so, for the most part, in order to turn the small compensation over to a hospital.

I must protest the report that I received "cries of indignation and letters of protest." Such was not the case. The protest, in this case, should be directed to the editors of LIFE for such poor copy and nondescript pictures.

Sterling C. Morris
Town Manager
Camden, Maine

Under Morris's letter the editor added a note that seemed to back-pedal a little:

A quarter of the extras contributed their pay to a fund raising drive sponsored by the Friends of Camden Memorial Hospital. LIFE's reporter heard expressions of indignation from a number of Camdenites who said they were going to protest to the town manager. —ED.

Among the pictures in the *Life* story was one of *Peyton Place* actor Lloyd Nolan attending the Rockport High School Alumni Association dinner and reunion. Vere Crockett, who had been helping staff the movie's nerve center and casting extras, introduced Nolan as the guest speaker. Nolan outlined his life and talked about some of his unusual experiences. Nolan gave some facts about the movie *Peyton Place*. He answered questions and later gave out autographs. Nolan's talk was described as very interesting and amusing.

"Everyone had thoroughly enjoyed his remarks," reported Hall in the *Camden Herald*.

In the picture of that dinner that appeared in *Life*, there was an alumna named Diana W. Folger making remarks. The caption read, "VOICING AN OBJECTION, teacher Diana W. Folger outlines the horrors told in *Peyton Place* at the high school alumni dinner. Actor Lloyd Nolan, a guest at the dinner, looks uncertainly up at her."

Joe Badger, on the hospital building committee, felt he needed to address the *Life* story. Badger wrote a letter to the editors of *Life*, taking issue with several points in the story, but the letter did not appear in the magazine. No copy was made of that letter. Badger, however, did receive a response to his letter, dated October 17, 1957:

> Dear Mr. Badger:
>
> We regret that someone who cares as much about Camden as you obviously do should have received such an ugly impression of LIFE's reaction to your home town. LIFE never intended to imply all you unfortunately managed to read into our August 26 article. LIFE's reporter came back from his trip with nothing but praise for one of the nicest places he said he had ever visited. If you were able to infer from the story a patronizing or sarcastic attitude to your town, we assure you it was not consciously written in.
>
> We wish we could leave it at that. Inferences are a matter of opinion, and you are entitled to yours. But since you also accuse us of deliberate untruths, each of which we can refute, we feel we must answer this part of your letter point for point.
>
> To reply to your statement that "The town around which *Peyton Place* was written is not the least like Camden," and to defend ours that *Peyton Place* was written about a little New England Town "a lot like Camden" our reporter says he heard a dozen Camdenites verify the comparison unprompted. Included were a school master, a minister, members of both the summer and winter communities, and many of the younger generation. Many of these people defend Camden's acceptance of the movie as an act of local broadminded- ness that recognized Camden could not pretend to be any holier than the average New England town. All the above people agreed on something else, too: they loved their town.

Later on you quote the town manager as saying "not one letter or phone call of protest was ever received by me" in contradiction to our statement that there were protests to the town manager. But a minister told our reporter of one letter of protest to the manager, and two local people told him of their intention to protest. If these intentions were not carried out, then LIFE's statement was too strong. We are, however, in receipt of a letter from the town manager in which he admits he does indeed recall one protest.

Going on to your statement that the three men engaged in a tug of war were not residents of Camden but members of the 20th Century Fox crew, you are right. They are not residents of Camden, and we did not say they were.

In another place you say LIFE's reporter was never able to find a single person willing to say he objected to the picture being made in Camden. On the contrary, he found many dissenters his first day and in two weeks time found literally dozens in every walk of life, age bracket, and social level.

Finally, we come to our treatment of the teacher's speech at the alumni dinner in Rockport. We were aware that there is a smile on the lady's face as there is on almost everyone's face in the picture. She was indeed outlining the horrors of *Peyton Place* at the time, but she was doing it in the tongue-in-cheek manner of a person who took all this movie-making as it should be taken: with a grain of salt. Her horrendous catalogue ended by having everyone at the dinner in stitches. Our caption which you read too literally was written in the same tongue-in-cheek spirit.

You do make one complaint about which we are as regretful as you—that we could not include the full story of the extras and their contribution to the Friends of the Camden Community Hospital. But we are first of all a picture magazine, and, since none of the pictures we took of the CCH in action were strong enough to rate places in the layout, we decided that bringing up the hospital in the brief text available would only confuse our readers. As you probably know, we published this information in a subsequent letters to the Editors column—with an editor's comment.

A last word. Our omission was not for lack of awareness of the important role played by your group. Our reporter filed over forty pages of research on this story. But our reporters are trained to report on all aspects of an assignment as are our photographers. What we finally publish in the finished story form is the work and decision of our editors alone. Inevitably much that is of secondary significance to the main theme of an article has to be left out when space is limited as it was for this story. We are truly sorry the choices we made in this presentation so thoroughly displeased you, and hope this discussion has helped to modify some of your objections.

The letter was signed by Cecily Gemmell for the Editors. Mr. Badger responded in a letter dated October 21, 1957:

Dear Miss Gemmell:

I appreciate your replying, on behalf of the editors, to my recent letter. I note, however, that you did not see fit to publish it in your "Letters to the Editors" department.

It is probably useless to continue this correspondence but my conscience would not let me sleep if I did not reply.

Let's take that statement "a lot like Camden." You now say that your reporter gained that idea from some people who live here. I have no theory to explain why he should consider them authorities, or why *Life* so accepted them, for *Life* made a flat statement, not a quoted one. You also in your letter add, "they loved their town." May I ask if these two statements about Camden are the least bit logical taken together? If Camden was much like *Peyton Place* the only people who would love it would be either evil or imbeciles. If your reporter could find such people here, which I doubt, is it *Life's* policy to accept them as experts?

I quote your letter: "But a minister told our reporter of ONE (emphasis mine) letter of protest to the manager and TWO (emphasis mine) local people told him of their intention to protest." If these add up to *Life's* statement, "there were cries of indignation and letters of protest . . . " *Life* is indeed capable of the grossest exaggeration. The one letter of protest received by the town manager was not even from a native of this town.

As to the tug of war picture caption, your story from the beginning stressed the fact that Camden People were acting as extras. Would it not have been accurate reporting to say that these gross individuals were not typical of our citizens but 20th Century Fox employees, instead of letting the inference stand that they were Camden people?

It is curious that your reporter "found many dissenters his first day" when on his second or third day here he asked a friend of mine to help him find someone who was opposed, as he had found only people in favor up to that time. Perhaps John's memory is bad.

But the true peak of your letter is the paragraph about your picture of the teacher at the alumni dinner in Rockport. You say your caption "was written in the same tongue-in-cheek spirit." If you had your tongue in your cheek on that statement you must have kept it there while you twisted the rest of the captions and pictures to suit you.

Incidentally, and very much so, but as a further comment on the way *Life* does things, I gave, at your reporter's request, and at my expense, a dinner for members of the cast in my home, I was told that I would receive prints of the pictures taken. Of course they never arrived. And after the story ran I could understand that this was not out of line with *Life*'s usual method of doing things.

Very truly yours, Joseph L. Badger.

P.S. As one final example of *Life*'s inaccurate reporting, the mention in Letters to the Editors refers to Friends of the "Camden Memorial Hospital." No such hospital exists! Can't you even set a name straight? And you had my letter on a printed letterhead!

Ham Hall kept the citizens of Camden informed of the ongoing developments in the battle with *Life* magazine, reprinting all the correspondence in the *Camden Herald*.

Ironically, it was an announcement from Badger a few weeks later that would turn Camden's attention from the *Life* magazine article to something more positive. Badger shared the good news that Camden would, indeed, be host to the premiere of *Peyton Place*.

On November 8 Badger received a response to the letter and petition he had sent to Wald in Hollywood, requesting that Camden be the location of *Peyton Place*'s premiere.

Wald confirmed with Badger that the movie *Peyton Place*, the most talked-about movie of the year, would have its premiere not in New York or Hollywood but in the town where it was shot: Camden, Maine. The movie was offered free of charge from the studio for Camden's premiere night.

"In the twenty-five years I have made motion pictures, your letter was the most touching I have ever received," wrote Wald. "All of us in the picture business are continually trying to do more than our share to become an integral part of the world we live in. We go out of our way to give as much help as possible, but you'd be amazed at how few people are considerate enough to thank us, consequently your letter of thanks makes up for many, many letters we have never received."

Badger said he was told that all the scenes shot in Camden had been retained in the final version of the picture. It had originally been expected that only a small fraction would be. Furthermore: "It might interest you to know that the Legion of Decency gave us the highest possible rating for a film: an A2 rating," wrote Wald. "I feel certain that all the people who see *Peyton Place* will be as pleased with it as we are."

Seven

It is a picture to make you "Maine-proud."

—Rockland *Courier-Gazette*

HAM HALL hailed 20th Century Fox's decision to hold *Peyton Place*'s premiere in Camden:

Perhaps the most exciting local news of the week is the announcement from 20th Century Fox, producers of *Peyton Place* that the world Premiere of this much publicized film will be held in Camden Wednesday, December 11.

This generous gesture of this world known motion picture producer is the result of many factors. When this large group of technicians, directors and actors moved into the Penobscot Bay Region in early May to film background shots for a story which had met considerable controversy elsewhere, they soon found the people of this area friendly and cooperative. During the month or more that this large group was with us, many lasting friendships were made and it did not seem unnatural that the production crew received a request petition of six hundred names for a Camden premiere showing of the film, with approval.

There was of course, no assurance that this would be possible for in such a tremendous organization there are many channels through which a request of this nature must pass.

Word came through Friday that 20th Century Fox had decided to give a one day premiere to Camden for the benefit of this town's new Community Hospital Building Fund. It seems assured that the Hospital will receive several thousand dollars toward this goal as the result of 20th Century's decision. Thanks to the free offer of the film and only out of pocket expenses for the theater most of the take should be net profit.

Over and above the sum realized this area should benefit greatly from what we truly believe will be worthwhile publicity.

From sources in Hollywood we understand that this is considered the best picture since *Giant*, that the Maine scenic photography is wonderful and that the Legion of Decency has given the film an A rating.

It's unusual for such a small town, deserving as it maybe, to be able to travel in such big time even for a day.

So with grateful appreciation to our friends in 20th Century let's make the most of it.

A program, publicity, and ticket committee of Camden residents was set up, with Joe Badger in charge. The committee also consisted of Mrs. Badger, Mr. and Mrs. Ray Goodrich, Anita Montgomery, and Hamilton Hall.

Ticket orders were coming in from as far away as Rhode Island, Massachusetts, and New Hampshire as well as from all over Maine.

Proceeds were to go to the Camden Community Hospital Building Fund, and the event was expected to raise over $4,000. Two evening performances, one at 6:30 and one at 9:30 p.m., were scheduled for the Camden Theater. The theater was owned by the Graphic Theater Circuit of Boston, and they donated the use of the venue for the cause. Tickets cost five dollars and three dollars each, with 606 seats available. People were asked to send cash, check, or money order to Badger to order tickets.

The film would begin regular showings, the day after Camden's premiere, at the Roxy Theatre in New York City and the Theatre of the National Academy of Movie Arts and Sciences in Hollywood.

This would be Mainers' only chance to see the premiere for a while, as 20th Century Fox was only releasing it in a few large cities at a time.

At the time of the announcement, it was not known which stars would be there, but Badger was assured that if any of them were available, they would be.

Ultimately actors from the movie were unable to attend. The studio arranged for two acting legends, who happened also to be Mainers, to attend the premiere: Bette Davis and Gary Merrill.

Bette Davis was forty-nine at the time of the premiere of *Peyton Place*. She was a living legend. After an unsuccessful early acting career, she began to make her name in movies in the 1940s. She was known for taking on unpopular roles and making them her own. Twice she won an Academy Award for Best Actress. She was the first female president of the Academy of Motion Picture Arts and Sciences. She also helped organize the Hollywood Canteen.

Gary Merrill was forty-two when *Peyton Place* premiered in Camden. A native of Hartford, Connecticut, Merrill attended Bowdoin College in Brunswick, Maine. He had earned respect performing supporting roles in westerns, including *Twelve O'Clock High*. Merrill had also been starring in an NBC crime drama at the time of *Peyton Place's* premiere. He and Davis were married on July 28, 1950, the same day his divorce from his first wife was finalized. Merrill was politically active, including campaigning to elect Edmund Muskie as Maine governor. After being involved in the *Peyton Place* premiere, Merrill would seek nomination to the Maine legislature as an antiwar, pro-environmentalist primary candidate during the Vietnam War. In an effort to promote black voter registration, in 1965 he would also take part in the Selma-to-Montgomery marches. Gary Merrill died in Falmouth, Maine, and is buried in that city.

The *Republican Journal* of Belfast, where part of the movie had been shot, had no story about the Camden premiere.

Camden was described as buzzing all day in curious anticipation as December 11 rolled around. It must have been a magical time in Camden in December 1957. Thanksgiving was just a few weeks before, and Christmas was in the Maine air. The village, filled with its many shops, was all decorated for the upcoming holiday, as was the entire length of Main Street and beyond. The lampposts sported trimmed Christmas trees, and the storefronts were decorated with holiday trimmings. Even the good weather turned out for the glamorous evening.

"After two days of cold rain the sun came out, lighting the hills and the Bay, as though to prove to the twelve hundred paying customers who would see the picture that our beautiful scenery, against which much of the movie was filmed last summer, was for real and not just a trick of color photography," wrote Ham Hall in his commemorative edition of the *Camden Herald*.

The excitement that had accompanied the filming must have still been in the air as those Camdenites who served as extras waited to see if they had made it into a scene. Cary Cooper, Tamblyn's stand-in, had been let out of Bowdoin for the day to attend. Out-of-state press was in attendance (though not *Life* magazine). Ham Hall was there covering it for the *Camden Herald*'s special World Premiere Country Style edition. People came from neighboring states to attend the premiere. One person from Massachusetts had just happened to be going through Camden during filming and stayed a day or two because he was an amateur camera enthusiast. He came back for the premiere. After the local schools had let out that afternoon, prior to the premiere, crowds gathered in the high school auditorium for the extras party.

In the auditorium there were two bands playing: the high school band and a country band. The high school gym was described as a colorful sight. The fifty-piece Camden High School Band, led by Chester Hammond, had on their brilliant scarlet jackets and white trousers. Fishnets, lobster traps, a rowboat, and an old sea chest decorated the stage. On the walls around the room were attractive exhibits of local industries. Among the exhibitors were the Knox Marine Exchange, Sutton Supply, Penobscot Cabin Company, Harry Stump, Knox Woolen Company, Brewster Shirts, Camden Tanning Corporation, Wentworth Farms, *Down East* magazine, and Katherine Adams Studio.

A table of studio stills for sale was presided over by Ray Goodrich. The table was doing a brisk business.

Town Managers Sterling Morris and Archie Stevens were on the welcoming committee at the extras party, and Fred Crockett, executive secretary of the chamber of commerce, acted as master of ceremonies and introduced Bette Davis and Gary Merrill as they arrived.

After introducing Merrill, Crockett turned the podium over to Norman Cote, the manager of the IGA Foodliner. Cote introduced the rest of the program, which consisted of Jean Litchfield and Betsy Crockett doing a Charleston as well as the high school and country bands.

"Fred Crockett should get a medal for being the shortest-winded master of ceremonies on record. Bravo," wrote the Rockland *Courier-Gazette*.

Gary Merrill then auctioned off the director's chair used by Robson during the movie's shooting as well as the original movie script, which was bound in gold. Mr. and Mrs. George Pew of Falmouth bid on the script, as did Ham Hall. Secretly Hall represented a syndicate of three Camden residents and was bidding on the script for the purpose of donating it to the Camden Public Library. The Pews did not know that and began bidding against Hall. Before the auction was over, John Poland, of Camden, called out from the audience that the script should go to the library. In the end Pew said he would bid $105 if the library, which had refused to have the book *Peyton Place* on its shelves, would accept the script from him. There was resounding applause after the bidding ended and the Pews won. Pew then presented the script to the Camden Library, where it still resides. And Ham Hall and his fellow investors saved themselves a lot of money.

Mrs. Adelaide Adelmann, of Rockland, won the director's chair.

Gary Merrill and Bette Davis were then presented a pair of creamy-white Knox blankets and some red woolen Brewster shirts, by Fred Crockett.

"If Gary Merrill ever decides to give up acting, he could be a very successful auctioneer," said the Rockland *Courier-Gazette*. "He was excellent. And both he and his wife, Bette Davis, were gracious and friendly; a pleasure to have around. We hope they come back for more visits."

At five o'clock a cocktail party was held at the Broadlawn Inn with Emeline Paige and Janet Hutchinson as hostesses. Merrill and Davis attended.

Mr. and Mrs. Alexander Hardie of Camden assisted as hosts at a special reception that had also been arranged for news, television, and radio reporters at the Broadlawn Inn preceding the premiere.

A box lunch was served from 5:00 to 7:00 p.m. by the Tri-Hi-Yo Girls, under the direction of Marion Hopkins, the same woman who had made the fish chowder for the cast and crew party at the Camden Outing Club. A part of those proceeds would go to the hospital fund.

Then it was on to the Camden Theater for the show. A parade of cars with stars, distinguished guests, and representatives of Governor Muskie was expected to travel to the theater in a motorcade.

Agnes Gibbs, described as Maine's first lady of radio and television, was to conduct a fifteen-minute live broadcast immediately following the show, from 8:30 to 8:45 p.m. on WCSH. Cameras from television stations WABI, WCSH, WGAN, and WTWO were expected to be there.

At the theater the narrow street was roped off. Merrill and Davis made an entrance to the sound of clicking cameras. Inside they briefly introduced the extras and those who had worked to get the movie shot in town.

The movie house was filled to capacity well before 6:00 p.m. and was packed for both showings, with all seats reserved, standing room only. Before the start of the picture, Crockett introduced Merrill and Davis. The Merrills then introduced other prominent people in the audience. There were Fred Clough, head of the Maine Department of Economic Development, who brought a message of congratulations to Camden from Governor Muskie; Agnes Gibbs, of WCSH radio and television; Earl Doucette, the Maine state official who had helped locate the movie crew in the state; Gordon Langley Hall, an English-born journalist who had recently scooped the rest of the press on the story of the romance between England's Princess Margaret and a Captain Townsend, which was another scandalous story; accent coach Fred Perkins; Camden town manager Sterling Morris; and stand-ins Cary and Ellen Cooper. Finally journalist Jim Moore was introduced, and Bette Davis subjected him to the kind of questioning she said newspaper men frequently pull on celebrities, to the great amusement of the audience.

The ticket booth was staffed by Mrs. John Montgomery, Mrs. Joseph Badger, and Mrs. Ray Goodrich, from the Friends of the Camden Community Hospital, for the sale of last-minute tickets.

Some people complained about the ticket prices. The *Providence Journal* interviewed one member of the barbershop quartet that appeared in the movie.

"Too much money. Besides I can see myself shaving every morning, so why pay five bucks or ten? I couldn't go without my missus," the gentleman replied.

Inside the theater, as the movie started, *oohs* and *aahs* broke out in the opening scene that showed the harbor from the mountain, and they continued every time a different local landmark was shown. A reporter from the *Providence Journal* wondered if anyone was paying attention to the plot at all.

The scene in which the female sextet sings the unrehearsed "Sweet Genevieve" received the most applause.

"The home town audience got a good laugh when they saw the Greyhound bus supposedly heading for New York City take off up Main Street in the direction of Belfast," observed the *Camden Herald*.

Reaction to the movie that night was good. Applause broke out often throughout the showings. Reporters said folks would have a good time identifying friends and neighbors in the pictures that did make it into the story. Among the things said in the theater that night: "There's Jim. . . . Look at Bill. . . . Boy, there comes the band and all its discords. . . . There's Dick Moody."

At 8:30 Bette Davis and Gary Merrill had to leave the theater to head to the IGA for the live NBC interview. People waiting to see the second showing of the movie listened as they gave their description and impressions of the movie. When the interview was over, they were whisked back to the theater to see the rest of the movie.

Davis said she loved the movie: "It is the best cast picture I have ever seen, right down to the smallest bit part."

Camden and the surrounding areas looked beautiful as the backdrop for the opening shots and credits, as well as for a special effects backdrop for the scenes filmed in Hollywood. The beauty of that area of Maine helps solidify the recurring theme of nature that is presented throughout the movie, including what the movie called "a fifth season—of love."

The frequent wetting down of Main Street before filming shows up on the film. A few old cars are used repeatedly in many scenes.

There are the scenes that bring amusement to people watching the movie who have knowledge of the local geography—Allison starting to run to school in Camden, only to end up in Belfast, or the Greyhound bus that heads the wrong way to New York. It is ironic to see Camden's beautiful library in the movie, knowing the book from which the movie originated is not inside.

The scenes shot for Road's End hint of the past lives and secrets that linger in any small town. It is amusing to watch the scenes where Lana Turner is supposed to be in Maine, but instead viewers are watching the back of her stand-in.

The movie is fast-paced and is good storytelling, though not as good as the original book, which had more time to explore characters and their complicated relationships with one another. World War II plays a prominent part in the movie. In the book overactive teenager Rodney Harrington dies in a car accident; in the movie he dies in war. The best scene, it could be argued, is that of Dr. Swain telling the truth at the trial about Selena's lost pregnancy, his attack on gossip and narrow-mindedness.

The movie pays homage to the book's author, re-creating a famous picture of Grace Metalious that has always been called *Pandora in Blue Jeans*. This was a publicity picture for the book that shows Grace sitting hunched over a typewriter, a look of thought on her face, pounding out the book that would set America afire. In the movie, it is young writer Allison who is hunched over the old black typewriter.

And in the end, Allison, as in the book, does find her season of love. Marion F. French wrote a review in the *Camden Herald*:

Once upon a time there was an explosive book which flung the nation's readers into controversial fury both for what it said and the way in which it said it. In Hollywood a young producer took the book, cut cleanly to the heart of its story, wrapped it in an amazing assortment of penetrating performances, placed it in a tiny town whose scenic beauty is delighting millions and proved that the motion picture has no master when it chooses to meet a challenge. The challenge—*Peyton Place*.

Producer Jerry Wald has made out of *Peyton Place* a tribute to life and to youth. And it is youth, standing head and shoulders over veteran competition, who runs away with the picture, acting-wise.

Young Russ Tamblyn, in his first demanding role as the shy, mother-dominated, Norman Page, reveals a talent astounding in its sensitivity and appreciation. His character grows before your eyes winningly and with such appeal that the audience is impelled to urge him on, and did, with applause.

Diane Varsi, as winsome and suited to her casting as advance reports claimed, handled her long, difficult and varied role with dignity and beauty. Terry Moore, as the town flirt, accomplished more in her brief scenes to establish the counterpoint of the story than some whose roles ranged the length of the picture and her co-actor, Barry Coe, as the spoiled son of a wealthy manufacturer, was completely realistic.

Barry S. Coe played Rodney Harrington. Coe's father had been a writer and publicist for Warner Brothers. Coe was 23 when he came to Camden to film *Peyton Place*. He had been in mostly B movies and had a small role in the Elvis Presley classic "Love Me Tender." His part in *Peyton Place* was his first notable role.

Faced with this sort of work the veteran actors, Lana Turner, Lloyd Nolan, Hope Lange, Lee Philips and Arthur Kennedy have hard sledding. Of the group it is Arthur Kennedy and Lee Philips who emerge most effectively. Mr. Kennedy, as the revolting villain is chillingly true and he manages to cross the borderline from a sodden, pathetic drunk to vicious hate-ridden wreck most convincingly.

Lee Philips, as Michael Rossi, the school principal, gave the impression that of them all he was the only one who had read the original book. His was the role that was cut most clearly, yet such was his depth of approach that he managed to convey the personality of the original characterization completely. Lloyd Nolan was his usual quietly impressive best as Doc Swain and of all the cast he was the only one to master to any degree of conviction the "downeast drawl." For the most part the rest were nearer to the south. It is easy to spot the "local appearances" even though they are most skillfully blended into the scenes and for all the people of this area the opening gambit of the "man with the plow" is worth the entire price of admission.

It is thrilling to see one's state, its beauty and its attractions through new eyes. As each superb vista unfolds itself it awakens and gains one's appreciation. When this is combined with a superb mastery of a subject and an obviously sympathetic treatment, it is doubly endearing. *Peyton Place* deserves every accolade it will receive. It is a picture to make you "Maine-proud."

The Rockland *Courier-Gazette* published an unofficial review of the movie within a news item about the movie:

Peyton Place, which had its world premiere last night at the Camden Theater, was a visual treat from beginning to end. Thanks to superb color photography, the scenery in and around Camden, where much of the picture was filmed last summer, was always stunning and at times breathtaking.

The acting was equally excellent, so good it is difficult to single any one performer out, from the stars, Lana Turner and Lloyd Nolan, right on down. As Bette Davis, herself a winner of several Academy Awards for picture performances put it, "It is the best cast picture I have ever seen, right down to the smallest detail."

If we had to pick standouts, we would say Russ Tamblyn, playing the exceptionally well-written part of the teacher Mike Rossie, and Terry Moore as Betty Anderson, the rich boy's girlfriend, were tops of an all-topnotch cast. [Note: Russ Tamblyn played Norman Page, and Lee Philips played Mike Rossi.]

But this reporter found the same fault in the movie version that we had in the book, namely: it doesn't tell the whole story. Only a hypocrite would deny that what happens in *Peyton Place* could and does happen in both small towns and larger ones. And anyone who has ever been young knows what a difficulty sex can be in the teen years. Nevertheless, there are still *some* wholesome family relationships around. We hope; and it is hard to believe that any group of young people however curious and confused, would not take time out from petting occasionally for just plain kid fun. There was none of either in *Peyton Place*.

Essentially it is three stories in one. There is the story of Selena Cross, from the tar paper shack part of town, who is forced to submit to the attentions of a lecherous, alcoholic stepfather (he was her real father in the book) [Note: He was the real father in the manuscript, but he was changed to her stepfather for publication of the book.] which results in her pregnancy, and later in a murder. Then there is the story of Selena's best friend, Allison Mackenzie, and Allison's mother Constance, seemingly a paragon of rigid morality but who, it develops, had had her daughter without benefit of matrimony. And there's a sub-story about Roger Harrington, a rich man's spoiled son who is involved with a cheap little pepper-pot, whose ways hide her true-blueness.

In an early sequence Selena, a senior in high school, is shown getting dressed matter-of-fact before the bleary, lustful eyes of her step-father. We presume the script writer meant to establish by this her unself-consciousness and innocence. What it seemed to do, instead, was make a case for the brutish man who, for all his faults, could hardly be expected to be blind to the girl's allure, unconscious or otherwise. Surely at her age some instinctive modesty would have motivated her to draw the curtain without his calling attention to the need for doing so.

Another false note occurred when Dr. Swain decided to tell the whole truth at Selena's trial for the murder of her stepfather. While we don't quarrel with the decision, we suspect that in reality such sordid revelations would have been confined to the Judge's Chambers or at least a cleared courtroom, rather than told on the witness stand for all the world to know—and remember.

But this is splitting hairs. On the whole the picture is beautifully done. It is acted with moving warmth and sincerity by everyone in it. There are delightful directorial touches, like the running gag of Joey Cross eating everything in sight at the Labor Day Picnic. And the scenery is out of this world—unless, of course, you live in or around Camden, Maine.

Slice-of-life dramas, such as this, are every bit as important as prettier portrayals of the world we live in. But unless they are sensitively handled they tend to seem like glorified peep-shows. *Peyton Place* avoided this pitfall, thanks to the always compassionate direction of Mark Robson. The result is a warm, moving, and always eye-filling motion picture.

At the premiere in Camden, a reporter from the *Providence Journal* made note of the lack of stars at the premiere and then asked about the absence of the author of the book that had started it all. The reporter asked, "But what about the author, Grace Metalious? What if someone had at the end of the film cried 'Author-Author'? She was the one who really made it all possible. The merchants benefited from the publicity and the hospital building fund will get a fat check for around $6,000, as the proceeds of the ticket sales went to this fund."

The reporter had Metalious's phone number and called her in Laconia, New Hampshire. The phone was answered by T. J. Martin, Metalious's manager and boyfriend. Martin said Metalious was out picking up the children at school. The reporter asked Martin why Metalious had not been at the Camden premiere.

Martin said Metalious had been busy trying to come up with copy for her new book, *The Tight White Collar*, which would eventually become her fourth novel. Martin must have learned a thing or two from Grace Metalious during his time with the married mother of three. Martin must have learned that a tall tale that adds to the controversy surrounding *Peyton Place* always ended in profit.

Martin also said there was another reason Metalious was not at the premiere: "She wasn't invited."

Davis said she, herself, had called and invited Metalious. Later, Martin did say that Metalious was called personally by Bette Davis to invite the author but that Metalious did not take the call.

Eight

It was our first exposure to Hollywood.

—PETER STRANG, FILM EXTRA IN THE CUB SCOUT PARADE SCENE

*A*T THE NEXT meeting of the Friends of the Camden Community Hospital, it was announced that the premiere had netted $5,119.89 for the hospital building fund, and a check in that amount was given to Mrs. Earle Pitman. This was made up from $5,557 from ticket sales, $52 from the sale of pictures, $105 from the script auction, and $41 from the chair auction. The Friends also made $421 from a pool on the possible gross sales of pictures, from which the $10 prize was granted immediately. The total proceeds, after donations from some of the extras, were over $6,000.

"This was truly a community effort. To mention all the individuals who contributed their time and effort would be like publishing a telephone directory," wrote the *Camden Herald*.

A former resident of Camden, Carl Hopkins, who had moved to Montpelier, Vermont, expressed his view of the movie. It was Hopkins's brother who designed the arch at the entrance to town where the first scene was shot. Carl Hopkins wrote a letter to the *Camden Herald* dated December 24, 1957:

> As a subscriber of the *Herald* for a great many years and a former Camden boy, I was particularly interested in last week's issue which

concerned the filming and premiere showing of *Peyton Place,* so much so that I gave my copy to the editor of our local paper the *Montpelier Evening Argus.* This resulted in the final editorial in the copy enclosed. . . .

I grew up in Camden and graduated from C.H.S. in 1910. I am very proud of my home town and the lively public spirit of its citizens which should be an outstanding example to other towns. I am particularly proud of my late brother Adin, whose unselfish devotion of time and talent to the civic affairs of the town was a notable contribution. I shall always cherish the memory of the generous tributes paid him at the time of his passing.

Please accept my kindest regards and very best wishes for continued success and prosperity of yourself, your paper and all the good people of Camden.

Most sincerely, Carl H. Hopkins

Vermont having rejected the movie company's offer to shoot in their state, the *Montpelier Evening Argus* wrote an editorial, at Hopkins's request, regarding Camden and *Peyton Place*'s filming. Ham Hall ran the clipping Hopkins had sent him, in the *Camden Herald.*

The controversial novel *Peyton Place,* the story of life in a small town, which has been called obscene and banned in some places, has turned out to be of great benefit to Camden, Maine. The world premiere of the motion picture made from the book, was held in Camden for the benefit of the community hospital there and netted $5,000 for the improvement of that institution. . . .

By the way, the film has been given the Legion of Decency's high A-2 rating and is considered a top candidate for the Oscar award. If it's a winner even greater fame will come to Camden and vicinity—and it would amount to an Oscar for Maine's scenery. The Hollywood group who filmed the picture last summer were pleased with the reception in Maine and may be influential in bringing further movie-making to the state. That is the hope of Maine officials.

Shortly after *Peyton Place* premiered in Camden, Governor Muskie sent a twenty-seven-foot Maine balsam fir to the people of Southern California. The tree was chosen by a committee of experts of the Maine Christmas Tree Growers Association and was flown by the Flying Tiger Line to Burbank Airport. It was received by Hope Lange and Barry Coe, two of *Peyton Place*'s stars.

The tree was going to be donated to the UCLA Medical Center Hospital. Wald sent a note along with the tree to that facility. Wald said he was asked by the people of Camden to express their thanks for the generosity of 20th Century Fox for making it possible for the fund-raising for the proposed community hospital.

"May this Christmas Tree fulfill its destiny, remind all who pass it of our individual and collective responsibility to bring peace on earth and good will towards all men," wrote Wald.

In early January the following year, the Board of Trustees of the Camden Public Library formally accepted the leather-bound movie script that had been won during bidding on the night of the premiere. The script was signed by Wald.

The acceptance committee consisted of A. Murray Austin, James Adams, Clayton McCobb, Elmer Wadsworth, Marion Long, Ruth Perry, Eleanor Guckes, Hope Gillmor, and Emma Alden.

A display case was prepared. It was the library's plan to display the script under glass and to turn the pages every once in a while. The script would not be available for circulation.

In a letter dated January 22, 1958, Wald wrote a letter to Hope P. Gillmor, secretary of the Camden Public Library: "Thank you for your kind letter of January 8th. I am delighted that the script of *PEYTON PLACE* is in the Camden Public Library, where it most certainly belongs."

The Camden Public Library also sent a thank-you letter to George Pew to thank him for his kindness in donating the script that he had won.

On January 27 Wald responded to a letter from Mrs. Herman A. Lowe, of 118 Chestnut Street in Camden:

Thank you very much for your nice letter of January 23rd and the review you were kind enough to send from the *Bangor Daily News*, which was excellent. It is unfortunate that Lana Turner's name was omitted from Elinor Hughes' review in the *Boston Herald* as I agree she gave a fine performance in *Peyton Place*.

The hope you voiced about the picture being a smashing success has already come true. It is doing fabulous business everywhere and I have had hundreds of letters asking where the film was shot, so Camden should be having a brisk tourist trade this summer. . . .

With the very best wishes to all the fine citizens of Camden, including yourself, of course, I am Jerry Wald.

In January 1958 *Peyton Place* opened for a week's run at the Bangor Opera House. The movie received generally favorable reviews, but not always. A review from the entertainment publication *Variety* was typical of many reviews: "In leaning backwards not to offend, Wald and Hayes have gone acrobatic. . . . On the screen is not the unpleasant sex-secret little town against which Grace Metalious set her story. These aren't the gossiping, spiteful, immoral people she portrayed. There are hints of this in the film, but only hints." *Variety* said that the acting was impressive and the cast was excellent, but it took exception at losing the heart of Metalious's book.

The *Monthly Film Bulletin* wrote, "Slick and passionless, the film is an expensive and heavily bowdlerized adaptation of Grace Metalious' best-seller. . . . The film never quite makes up its mind whether to extol small-town America or castigate it."

Peyton Place earned nine Oscar nominations in 1958:

Motion Picture: Jerry Wald
Director: Mark Robson
Actress: Lana Turner
Supporting Actress: Diane Varsi
Supporting Actress: Hope Lange
Supporting Actor: Arthur Kennedy
Supporting Actor: Russ Tamblyn
Writing: John Michael Hayes
Cinematography: William Mellor

In March, before the Oscar winners were announced, Camden held its own Oscar party. The award, contrived by the Camden-Rockport Chamber of Commerce, was a Brewster—a famous Knox all-wool jacket, "grown, spun, woven, and manufactured in Camden by the J. Brewster Shirt Co., Inc. for the past 65 years." On March 6, a Brewster jacket was sent to each of *Peyton Place*'s Academy Award nominees.

Each jacket included a certificate that read:

This certifies that _____ (star's name) who was nominated for an Oscar, has definitely won Camden's Oscar, which is a "Brewster"— grown, spun, woven, and manufactured in Camden—for the _____ (name of category) of 1957 in *Peyton Place* . . . from the people of Camden, Maine by the Camden-Rockport Chamber of Commerce.

Each certificate was signed by C. E. Waterman Jr., chamber of commerce president.

A special Brewster was sent to Don Prince, the movie's publicity man, for his work in having the premiere located in Camden and his continuing efforts to publicize Camden as the locale in the picture— "and because everyone who worked with him when he was here for 20th Century liked him," wrote Ham Hall.

Don Prince would send a letter of thanks to the chamber of commerce on behalf of everyone involved in the shooting. Twentieth Century Fox released a picture of Varsi receiving Camden's "Brewster" award from Wald. Included in the letter was a certificate that had been drawn up by the studio:

> To Whom It May Concern,
> Be it known to all men by these present that the 1958 20th Century Fox Studio Award for the best cinematic location of the year is hereby awarded to the town of Camden, Maine, that played with such grace and beauty the town of Peyton Place in the motion picture of that name.

The certificate was signed by Wald.

On January 27, 1958, it was announced that Varsi, nineteen, had filed for divorce from her husband, James Dickson, twenty-six, an independent movie producer. She claimed he inflicted "grievous bodily injury and grievous mental suffering" on her. They had been married only a few months before Varsi came to Maine for filming.

Diane Varsi was the youngest cast member to appear in Camden at the time of filming. Growing up she was considered an oddball and a rebel. At age fifteen she had dropped out of high school. Varsi was poor before coming to Hollywood, working as an apple picker, salesgirl, and assembly hand in a candle factory. She said she was also a wandering folk singer. Though her acting experience was limited, Varsi beat several famous actresses for the part of Allison MacKenzie. Her fellow actors at Fox described her as a frightened, bird-like girl who was bewildered by her sudden success. She and Russ Tamblyn would date briefly after the movie was shot. During the filming of Varsi's next movie, she reportedly had a nervous breakdown. She then left Hollywood.

In contrast to Varsi's promising, upcoming career, this was the first movie in which Lana Turner portrayed a mother.

According to Lloyd Shearer in a story in *Parade* magazine three months after *Peyton Place*'s premiere, a studio executive told him, "See those two girls on the screen? Well, Lana typifies all the evils of the 'old' Hollywood; Diane typifies all the virtues of the 'new' Hollywood." Wrote Shearer,

> Now as she approaches 40, Lana Turner is compelled to face facts: her appeal is limited primarily to members of her own generation— who apparently prefer free TV fare to movie houses; her screen future may be confined to matronly roles; the peak of her popularity has passed. Lana Turner is a classic example of what the old Hollywood has done to a beautiful, poor, impressionable, fun-loving girl.
>
> Diane Varsi, on the other hand, stands on the threshold of stardom. This tall (5'7", 120 pounds), blue-eyed blonde today occupies roughly the position Lana Turner held in 1935: she faces a golden future.

Turner had not originally wanted to be in *Peyton Place*. Twentieth Century Fox suggested Jane Wyman or Olivia de Havilland in the role of Constance MacKenzie. Turner was convinced to do the movie after Wald pointed out the success of Hollywood legend Joan Crawford as a mother in the movie *Mildred Pierce*.

Turner had agreed to take a percentage of the profits versus a salary for appearing in *Peyton Place*. She felt that Constance Mackenzie was not one of her better roles.

Ironically, it was the night of the Academy Award's Oscar ceremony in the spring of 1958, in which *Peyton Place* did not win a single award, that Lana Turner was cast into her biggest drama. Before the filming of *Peyton Place* began, Turner had started dating Johnny Stompanato, a mobster. For the next year they had a tumultuous relationship, with several breakups and just as many reconciliations. On March 26, 1958, returning from the Oscar ceremony that night, Stompanato assaulted Turner physically. She told him to leave her house. A week later he arrived at her rented house in Beverly Hills. There was an argument between the two, and Stompanato threatened to kill the star, her daughter, and her mother. Daughter Cheryl, who was watching television in a nearby room, came out and stabbed Stompanato with a kitchen knife. Turner called a doctor, who tried to revive the gangster but could not and called emergency services. Later that night Cheryl surrendered herself to the Beverly Hills Police Department. She was fourteen at the time. More than one hundred reporters attended the near-riotous inquest. In court

Stompanato's family would accuse Turner for being responsible for the killing and having her daughter take the blame. By the end of the day, the jury judged the killing to be justifiable homicide. However Cheryl was released to the custody of her grandmother because of the court's concerns about her current parental supervision. Turner was accused of putting on a performance during the inquest. *Life* magazine printed a picture of Turner from the inquest next to various movie roles in which she played scenes on a witness stand, including *Peyton Place*.

Diane Varsi died in 1992 at the age of fifty-four of respiratory problems. She also suffered from Lyme disease, according to her daughter, Wilo Hausman. Ironically, when she walked out on her contract with 20th Century Fox, she moved to Bennington, Vermont, one of the states that would not allow *Peyton Place* to be shot.

Wald would spend the rest of his life bragging about the deal he made in securing the rights to *Peyton Place*. Wald called the movie "no work of art, but a good movie and a hell of a money-maker."

Grace Metalious said that she was pleasantly surprised with the movie but thought it was sugar-coated. She found the rape scene tremendous. She thought Lana Turner was good, Lloyd Nolan was great, and Lee Philips was terrible. She thought Hope Lange was good but did not look like Selena.

"Allison came through fine," said Metalious of her book's main character.

Wald would call Metalious for a sequel to *Peyton Place*. He said he wanted a twenty-five-page synopsis, which he would turn into a movie. Metalious had vowed never to talk to Wald again after her experience in Hollywood for her two weeks as *Peyton Place*'s "script consultant." But her manager and boyfriend, T. J. Martin, told her that the money from her first book was gone, they needed the money from a sequel, and the money Wald offered was good for the small amount of work that she would need to do. Metalious wrote the book in thirty days.

The head of Dell Publishing, Helen Meyer, said, "Grace turned in something so terrible that it wasn't publishable."

Martin said that he estimated that almost half of *Return to Peyton Place* needed rewriting. He said the book appeared to be written by two different people: the Grace who was drinking and the Grace who was not.

Warren Miller was hired to "fix" the book. *Return to Peyton Place* sold three million copies in three weeks in the paperback editions, but the book came out to bad reviews.

"While Mrs. Metalious' preoccupation is still with sex, her language has lost some of its brash frankness and become more muted," wrote Rose Feld for the *New York Herald Tribune*.

"That book is just so much sludge; it was written for the 'gentlemen' of Hollywood who will do anything to make a quick buck," said Metalious. "I wish that I had never let it happen."

Attitudes in New Hampshire had changed toward the author. Perhaps it was Camden's positive experience with Metalious's first book. Though the movie was not filmed on location, Laconia wanted the premiere of this movie, and they contacted Metalious for help: "If Gilmanton can't have it, Laconia should be the next choice. Letters still appear in local paper. Interest high. Main streeters want *Peyton Place*. Chamber will cooperate. Do what you can."

Metalious promised Wald a five-city publicity tour for the movie if the premiere would be held in Laconia. Wald agreed. He promised Metalious that four stars from the movie would attend the premiere.

On April 27, 1961, *Return to Peyton Place* premiered in Laconia. Metalious was bitterly disappointed in the event.

A cheap mimeographed invitation had been sent out by 20th Century Fox to Metalious's guest list. A few Fox officials were at the premiere, as was a reporter from *Silver Screen* magazine. There were no movie stars.

Return to Peyton Place received more promotion from the movie studio than had the original movie because it did not sell itself the way *Peyton Place* had—there just wasn't the same controversy.

The premiere was held in Laconia on a beautiful spring evening, and the movie was well received. The premiere was called a bit of a reconciliation between Gilmanton and Metalious.

In June 1961 Wald announced a third *Peyton Place* project, called *Peyton Place Revisited*, to be delivered first in novel form.

"Producer Wald has already packed author Grace Metalious back to New Hampshire to soak up local off-color," reported *Time* magazine.

In 1962 Metalious produced two chapters of *Peyton Place Revisited*, along with an outline that would seal Allison's future and left no room for a sequel. The project was never finished. Instead Metalious published her next novel, *No Adam in Eden*. Twentieth Century Fox bought the rights to *No Adam in Eden*, but the movie was never made. The book met with mixed reviews, including this sharp one from *Newsweek*:

Grace Metalious has done it again! Yes, fans, the sensational author of *Peyton Place* has run another one through her typewriter, just the way you like it. . . . But you'd better hurry. The author's supply of talent is strictly limited.

Success did not pave a smooth road for Metalious. After *Peyton Place* was published, she was in a car accident with her mother in the car. Her mother sued her because of the accident. Metalious also learned that her agent had stolen money from her and that she owed back taxes. A lien was put on her house.

In October 1960 Metalious and Martin divorced, and two days later she remarried George. Two years later the *Boston Record* announced that Grace and George had again separated.

Toward the end of her life, with alcohol her only constant companion, Metalious announced that she was getting out of the book business. She said, "If I had to do it over again, it would be easier to be poor. . . . Before I was successful, I was as happy as anyone gets."

Metalious would meet journalist John Rees in 1963 and become involved with him. Rees was married, with children, but his family was back in England. On Tuesday, February 25, 1964, Metalious died alone at Beth Israel Hospital in Boston. Her family had not even known she was sick. She had changed her will the day before she died, leaving everything she had to Rees instead of to her own children. On her deathbed she reportedly said, "Darling, be careful of what you want. You may get it."

Because Metalious had left Rees everything, there was a fight between her family and him. The Metalious family wanted there to be a funeral, and Rees said Metalious did not want one. The fight went all the way to the New Hampshire Supreme Court, and in the end, the court ruled that the family had the right to Metalious's body. Her funeral quickly turned sensational. The family received calls that the author should not be buried at the Gilmanton cemetery where she now lies.

Rees ultimately gave up his claim on Metalious's estate. When all was tallied, Metalious ended up owing money. Her house and belongings were auctioned off. George Metalious wrote a biography of his wife shortly after she died, after a fight with Rees over book rights to her life.

Peyton Place is still run in Camden from time to time, and the event of the filming of *Peyton Place* is still observed.

Barbara Dyer, who serves as Camden's town historian, was opposed to *Peyton Place* being filmed in Camden at the time. In those days, she said, she worked at Wayfarer Marine and did not want to get caught up in the hoopla that overtook the town in 1957.

At the time of filming, a coworker suggested she read the book.

"That might be your idea of good literature, but it sure isn't mine," Dyer responded.

In 2007 Camden held a celebration to mark the fiftieth anniversary of the filming of *Peyton Place*. Metalious's two daughters, Marsha Metalious Duprey and Cynthia Metalious, attended the dinner, along with Christopher Murray, son of Hope Lange. The festivities were kicked off at a buffet dinner at the Whitehall Inn, which was used in the 1957 filming, and was attended by some of the people who served as extras. The parade scene was re-created, with vintage cars. The parade went from Main Street to the former Knox Woolen Mill. There was a brief photo opportunity at the mill, a screening of the movie at the Camden Opera House, and a panel discussion. Camden residents lined Main Street for the event.

"She would have been happy to have been invited now," said Marsha Duprey of her mother.

Camden resident Terry Bregy worked on the 2007 anniversary celebration, including narrating a special trolley organized for the event. Bregy was a summer resident of Camden at the time of the filming but was at summer camp when the production took place. The movie, however, led to his decision to live full-time in Maine.

"There was a real sense of pride in the portrayal of our natural beauty and small-town charm," said Bregy. "It was one of the reasons I moved here after college."

Charlene Strang, her son Peter Strang, and Sylvia Hawkins talked at the dinner about their experiences as extras.

"I wore a wide-brim hat for the graduation scene at the library amphitheater," said Hawkins. "I sat beside Lloyd Nolan, and he was very quiet. Finally, he turned to me and said, 'It's a lovely day.'"

Hawkins said the wide-brimmed hat kept her face from showing in the movie.

"So I'm still not in the film."

Peter Strang appeared as a Cub Scout marching in the parade scene.

"It was a lot of fun, and we had a lot of pride being in the den and being in the movie. It was our first exposure to Hollywood."

Jay Foster remembers the slight that was offered by the movie's star, Lana Turner, whose promised presence was continually dangled before the people of Maine but who never set foot in the state.

Foster said the feeling was that Turner was too good to come to a small town in a rural state. He said the people of Camden never forgave Turner and that her absence also hurt the overall look of the movie.

"I think everyone understood that the interior scenes in the house on Chestnut Street and in the Tweed Shop downtown were better shot on a soundstage in a controlled environment, but the outside scenes on Library Hill, outside the house, at the July 4th celebration, etc., would have been much better if shot real time instead of with a film backdrop of Camden shot on that same sound stage," said Foster.

When Foster saw the movie years after its shooting, he found the movie to be well done and said it brought back a lot of memories, of his own childhood and of Camden, the town he calls home.

"It was thrilling. You got to see the old Camden," said Foster. "It's fun watching the movie and how it's changed."

Foster said that when his now-adult children watch *Peyton Place,* they get an appreciation of what Camden used to be like.

"All that stuff was Camden," said Foster.

Foster said he has not read *Peyton Place.* He said the book's story line did not have much to do with what was filmed in Camden. Foster feels the filming of the movie did not change Camden in the long run.

"It was an event rather than character-changing," said Foster. He said the movie reached out and touched a lot of people in Maine. He still looks back on his part in *Peyton Place* in a positive way.

"It's always been fun to tell people I was in the movie *Peyton Place,*" said Foster. "That summer was a special summer."

Camden, Rockport, Rockland, Lincolnville, and Belfast, Maine had taken a chance in 1957 when they invited 20th Century Fox to film a controversial book in their towns. This was an economic opportunity: an opportunity for national publicity of the rural Maine scenery and perhaps another revenue stream for the state, as a movie location.

But it was also a stand about cultural freedom. It was a stand against narrow-mindedness and judgment. And it was a risky stand to take. Had the producers of the movie kept a little more of the original book content in the movie, Camden, the Maine town most associated with the filming, might have easily become shunned and marked by infamy. Without *Peyton Place's* script in hand, many people in the state took that courageous stand, and in the end, it would seem that the state of Maine and the people of the Camden area were rewarded with publicity and fame.

Edith Crockett, the Camden-Rockport Chamber of Commerce secretary who had been instrumental in bringing Hollywood to Maine in 1957, was one of many who had taken a gamble on 20th Century Fox.

Crockett was asked what she thought of the movie that had focused so much attention and controversy on her small Maine village.

"It is a movie version of an average small New England town with elements both good and bad," said Crockett. "How good or how bad should depend, we would think, upon your imagination."

LIST OF CAMDEN LOCATIONS

- Village Restaurant: Mike Rossi pulls up outside this restaurant when he first enters town.
- The Village Shop: Featured in the background and in Main Street shots.
- Tweed Shop: Constance MacKenzie's dress shop in the movie.
- Smiling Cow: Featured in Main Street scenes. Allison MacKenzie and Norman Page stand under its red-and-white-striped awning during the Labor Day parade.
- Boynton-McKay Drug Company: Featured in background and Main Street scenes.
- Haskell and Corthell and The Woman's Shop: In the background of Main Street scenes, noticeable when Rodney Harrington is in his car outside the Tweed Shop.
- Stevenson's Luncheonette and Candy Shop: Featured in background shots of Main Street.
- Brown's Market: Featured in background shots of Main Street.
- Camden Rexall Drug Store: The Greyhound Bus Stop was at this corner, where Allison leaves for New York City.
- D. E. Crockett's 5 and 10: Featured in background shots of town and Main Street.
- Libby's Pharmacy: Featured in background shots of Main Street.
- Allen's Insurance Agency: Featured in background shots of Main Street.
- The Hedgeman Store: Featured in background shots of Main Street.
- Dougherty's: Featured in background shots of Main Street.
- Achorn's: Featured in background shots of Main Street.

- Camden Public Library: Featured in Main Street scenes, especially as Mike Rossi enters town. Allison and Norman walk by the library on their way to Norman's house.
- Camden Amphitheater: Site of the high school graduation and Easter morning church services.
- Public Landing: This is the location for the part of the Labor Day celebration. Mike and Connie visit a fisherman along the waterfront.
- Jason Westerfield residence: Allison and Norman walk by this house and its wrought iron fence on their way to Norman's house.
- Monument Square: Mike Rossi drives by this square on his way into town. The Civil War Statue has since been moved to Harbor Park, and the square has been reconfigured.
- Dean Fisher residence: Doc Swain's house.
- Village Green: Featured in background shots and Main Street.
- Smart residence: The MacKenzie house.
- Chestnut Street Baptist Church: Used in the Sunday morning church sequence.
- Our Lady of Good Hope Catholic Church: The sign for this church was used in the Sunday morning church sequence.
- First Congregational Church of Camden: Used in the Sunday morning church sequence.
- Methodist Church: Used in the Sunday morning church sequence.
- Flanagan residence: Allison passes through this backyard on her way to school and stops to speak to Mrs. Flanagan and her son.
- Camden-Rockport Archway: This archway was changed to read "Entering Peyton Place" for the movie. Mike Rossi drives under this arch as he enters town.
- Mirror Lake: Off Route 17, it's called Crystal Pond in the movie.
- Whitehall Inn: The hotel and bar that Allison goes to when she returns for Selena Cross's trial.
- Knox Woolen Mill: Harrington Mills in the movie. The mill pond was also used for some of the Labor Day celebration scenes.
- Curtis Island and Lighthouse: Mike and Connie visit the lighthouse on their Labor Day outing.
- George W. Brown residence: Mike Rossi's house on the water, where Allison visits him.
- Mount Battie Trail: Allison takes Norman to her "secret place" at the top of Mount Battie.

SCENE LOCATIONS FROM TOWNS AROUND CAMDEN

- The Lobster Pound Restaurant on Route 1, Lincolnville Beach: Mike and Connie enjoy a lobster dinner here on Labor Day.
- Crosby School, Church Street, Belfast: Peyton Place High School.
- The First Church, Church Street, next to the Crosby School, Belfast: This was Allison's and Selena's church.
- Maine District Courthouse, Church Street, across from the First Church, Belfast: Peyton Place Hospital.
- St. Francis of Assisi Catholic Church, Court Street, Belfast: Used for interior church scenes and in the Sunday morning church sequence.
- Rockland District Courthouse, Union Street, Rockland: The courthouse where Selena Cross's trial was held.
- St. Bernard's Roman Catholic Church Statuary, Broadway, Rockland: Used in the Sunday morning church sequence.
- Thorndike Hotel, corner of Tillson and Main Streets, Rockland: The actors stayed here during filming.

SOURCES

Associated Press
Bangor Daily News
Boston Herald
Boston Traveler
Bregy, Terry, personal interview
Camden Herald
Camden Public Library
Camden Reporter
Chicago Tribune
Daily Kennebec Journal
Dyer, Barbara, personal interview
Foster, Jay, personal interview
The Girl from Peyton Place, George Metalious and June O'Shea, Dell
    Publishing Co., Inc., 1965.
Inside Peyton Place, Emily Toth, Doubleday and Company, 1981;
    reprinted by the University of Mississippi Press.
Lewiston Sun Journal
Life magazine
Look magazine
MaineToday.com
Manchester Union
Montgomery, Ann, correspondence with author
Monthly Film Bulletin
Montpelier Evening Argus
Newsweek
New York Herald Tribune

New York Times
Newsweek
Parade magazine
Peyton Place, Grace Metalious, Messner, Inc., 1956
Peyton Place (script), John Michael Hayes, 1957
Portland Press Herald
Providence Journal
Republican Journal
Rockland *Courier-Gazette*
Time magazine
VillageSoup.com
Unbuttoning America: A Biography of Peyton Place, Ardis Cameron,
    Cornell University Press, 2015
Variety
Walsh History Center, Camden, Maine